Songs
Against the Darkness

Dr. Stewart Bitkoff

Abandoned Ladder

Copyright © 2020 by Stewart Bitkoff

goldpath@ptd.net

Except as permitted under U.S. Copyright Law, no part of this book may be reprinted, reproduced, transmitted, or utilized in any form by any electronic, mechanical, or other means, now known or hereafter invented, including photocopying, microfilming, and recording, or in any information storage or retrieval system, without written permission from the publisher.

Printed in the United States of America

ISBN-13: 978-0-9915775-4-5

10 9 8 7 6 5 4 3 2 1

Introduction

In each day there is darkness and Light; this is the interplay of opposites working together to enhance our experience of multi-dimensional living. At the time of this writing, our world is experiencing great suffering, death and fear; everyone caught in a pandemic which is threatening hundreds of millions physically, emotionally and economically. Nations struggle caring for their ill and dying, and quarantining their citizens, while trying to maintain routine daily services. For the average person, each day is a struggle, being apart from others through illness or social distancing, and connecting through their common fear and frailty.

According to some, we are living at the end of one spiritual age — a tumultuous, chaotic time

— which is transitioning into another; a more enlightened period where the storm will have cleared the way for a new day. Until this morning arrives what are we to do?

When the storm is raging, the cold wind is blowing and the rain/snow is hitting our face, it is time to duck and take cover. Find shelter, make our self and family as safe as possible and wait out the storm. During this dark time to help ease our fear and offer guidance, here are some songs to sing.

Enclosed in this volume are 3 different pieces of writing. In Book One, 'Rosetta's Stone' is a dark novelette that follows Rosetta as she takes a retrospective look at her life. She is awaiting the arrival of her 2 sisters who she hasn't seen in years and memories of both dark and enjoyable times fill her mind. Next in Book Two, is a collection entitled 'Raising A Candle' which offers 60 poems and short pieces examining the interplay of darkness and Light. Last in the Appendix, there is an article 'How to be Spiritual Amidst this Chaos' which presents spirituality as a tool to help get through chaotic times.

When I worked in summer camp and the weather didn't permit normal outdoor activity, because the storm was raging, we gathered all the campers together in the field house and entertained each other with skits and singing. For a time, the energy of hundreds coming together in laughter and music lifted our spirits. Sometimes, we pitted one section against another in a song competition or staff who were musically skilled performed favorites. This activity helped us feel connected and renewed our energy.

    I hope you enjoy the written variety contained in this volume, and the different pieces help make your day a little brighter.

Dr. Stewart Bitkoff

Beyond the Pain

So, if God/Light created everything in the universe that means God created pain, illness, death and all manner of natural calamities.

And if men are God's representative on earth and must make a moment by moment choice between darkness and Light, why is life structured this way?

The wise claim this friction exists to push us forward so we might transcend the day to day and embrace that which lies beyond this world of forms.

And once this connection is forged, and love enters, it cannot easily be broken.
—SB

Book One:

Rosetta's Stone

Introduction

According to one philosophy this world is a giant bazaar filled with wonder, experience and opportunity. You will find in this world exactly what you desire; and the overall goal of life is to learn, change and grow in spiritual understanding.

Further we do this by recognizing who we wish to become and identifying what thoughts, attitudes and behaviors limit and stand in the way of this happening. Then we change these aspects by substituting others that help us reach higher.

In 1799 in the town of Rosetta, Egypt, a black, basalt stone tablet was discovered. It bore parallel writing in both Greek and Egyptian hieroglyphic characters; in time linguists and archaeologists used these parallel inscriptions to understand the hieroglyphic writings on the numerous ancient Egyptian buildings, temples and pyramids. Prior to this discovery, the meaning of these hieroglyphic writings had been lost and people struggled to understand them.

Similarly, each person's life is filled with a variety of puzzling, difficult to understand and seemingly unrelated events. Some of these experiences are joyful while others are full of pain. Some are sought after for years and others without notice select us. Yet there is a pattern and experience provides the opportunity to learn, grow and change; once the lesson is learned we evolve into a more advanced version of our self.

In this present piece, Rosetta through the various snapshots of past events, in part is reviewing life experience, and on an inner level is trying to identify what learning occurred. Often to understand and make sense out of our life experience, we require a key or Rosetta Stone. This is the higher, hidden magical piece and Rosetta is looking for a personal answer to understand her own life and behavior.

Fortunately, in this journey we are both the question and answer. The capacity to make sense out of life, to learn and change is deep within each waiting to be discovered and used. Also, to assist us we have the help of friends, family, religion and spiritual teachings.

How to begin to unravel the mystery of life experience and begin the process of purposeful change, in part, is the subject of this tale.

Please remember the characters in this story are fictional composites. Their resemblance to others is unintentional and any similarity is offered as a literary device.

May you enjoy this story.

Dr. Stewart Bitkoff

"I never felt as alive as when I was raising my three sons. This was a time when I was happiest."
    Rosetta B., 1978

Table of Contents

Introduction	xi
List of Characters	xvi
Chapter I- Rosetta's Stone	1
Chapter II- West 178th Street	12
Chapter III- Street Danger	46
Chapter IV- School Days	67
Chapter V- Rosetta's Blues	89
Chapter VI- Susquehanna Road	112

List of Characters

Rosetta B.: Main character.

Larry: Rosetta's husband.

Ellen & Martha: Rosetta's sisters, coming for a visit.

Papa Louie & Clara: Rosetta's father and second wife.

Ida: Papa Louie's first wife (deceased), Rosetta's birth mother.

Mr. Billy Silver: Television Evangelist.

Barry, Jet, Scott: Rosetta's 3 sons: Barry-3, youngest, Jet, middle-6 and Scott, eldest-10 years.

Edna: Rosetta's neighbor and friend, Manhattan, 1956.

Edna's Family: *Carrie*, daughter, 5 years, *Fred*, son, 10 years, *Mark*, husband.

Al: Rosetta and Larry's friend who is in love with Rosetta, Manhattan, 1956.

Synagogue Custodian: Manhattan, 1956.

Park Supervisor: Manhattan, 1956.

Building Superintendent: Manhattan, 1956.

Store Personnel:
Butcher, Manhattan, 1956.
Beverage Manager, Weegmain's

Rochester, 1984.
Joey, Supermarket Manager, Rochester, 1984.

Chapter I- Rosetta's Stone

Rochester, New York, 1984

Rosetta awoke still tired. Sitting on the edge of the bed, slowly she oriented herself to the new day. A night of tossing and turning had done little to relieve her low-grade head pain or ever-present fear and anxiety. She wondered where this unease came from. The headache was something new. As long as she could remember, worry had been part of her. Sleeping sometimes helped. Other times a few puffs from a cigarette or a glass of wine eased things. Last night each failed. Both the headache and worry persisted.

As Rosetta poured herself a cup of coffee, again she thought about her failure to adjust to the move from New York City; somehow, she could never be friendly with the people here. The people were kind and some had similar interests, but there was an ever-present awkwardness that lingered after every interaction. They did not share the same experience. Here the Jews were wealthy and belonged to another level of society. Larry never made enough money to join the country club and the few times they were invited, Rosetta felt like an outsider.

At first the move to Rochester seemed like a good idea. Larry moved up in the company and was promoted to run a small manufacturing plant outside of Palmyra. It took six months to get things set up with Larry traveling back and forth on weekends. This was an exciting time and finally the family moved into their own home; no more apartment living and for the first time money was not a problem.

Unfortunately, this did not last long. Due to poor business decisions by the owners, the company went belly-up and Larry had to find another job. Luckily, he was only out of work for three months and found work close by coordinating a warehouse for a local food distributor. The pay was not as good but included a regular salary and food discounts. These came in handy raising three teenage boys; you never have enough food in the house and when they brought their friends over, it took minutes to empty the refrigerator.

So much of the past couple of years was spent with heartache. First after the birth of the kids it was the 'blues.' Then sadness and ongoing arguments about moving away from the City; over time sadness turned to resentment and anger which she threw in Larry's face whenever she got upset. Which was often these days. It really wasn't right but she could not help herself. Larry asked before the move, if she wanted to go and like a good wife Rosetta said, "Yes." In the past she blocked many of Larry's plans and wanted to be supportive with this move. In hindsight, it probably would have been easier if they moved to Long Island like most of their friends and family.

This getting old 'was for the birds.' She didn't know who coined the term 'golden years' but in her view there was nothing 'golden' about them unless you were talking about some false teeth with that yellow metal in them. Every day another part of her body ached and much of their weekly schedule was tied-up going to doctors. Particularly if you had a chronic condition like heart disease or diabetes. Yes. The old people were right when they said, 'when you have your health you have everything.'

Also, Rosetta added, "In America it helped to have money as well." Life was certainly a whole lot easier when you didn't have to worry about your bills.

Rosetta stood by the window that overlooked the parking lot behind the garden apartments and lit-up a smoke. She took a deep drag and began to cough. Slowly she put the cigarette out in a nearby glass ashtray, took a seat at the kitchen table and felt her heart race. After the first heart attack, the doctors said, 'give up cigarettes and change your life.' She was told to diet and exercise, take heart medication and not smoke. 'Frig' the doctors, she thought. What did they know? She got enough exercise cooking and cleaning and barely ate anyway. Besides she was too sad to take care of herself and missed her family.

Rochester, 1984

Larry got into the place early and picked up enough samples to leave for the Managers of the local supermarkets. These were new items introduced into the line and were soon to be made available in the region. Having exclusive distribution had perks and Larry loved to keep the locals happy with freebies for their customers and themselves. This way, whenever Larry shopped for family groceries, there was something to talk about and the Managers looked out for him as well. Often he got the insider's price on items and free samples. These benefits helped stretch the dollar. Who could afford the price of meat and fish nowadays?

Larry drove down Monroe Avenue and passed their garden apartment. He knew Rosetta was probably awake by now and having morning coffee. He hoped that she would take her medication and not smoke so many cigarettes. When she made her mind up she could be very stubborn.

It had been hard, the move to Rochester. Even after 18 years, she still had not adjusted and was very lonely. She missed her sisters and their families. Finally, they sold their house and in a couple of months would begin the process of moving back to the City. Soon he would get Social Security and with the money they saved, they should be all right. Rosetta could pinch a penny with the best of them. They would look to live in Queens or Long Island; Manhattan had gotten too expensive and the Bronx had changed. The old Bronx neighborhood where they lived looked like a bomb hit it. Most of the stores were burnt out and people were shooting each other in the apartment buildings. Street drugs changed things; their old way of life in the Bronx was gone and replaced by a violent and more destructive one.

♦ ♦ ♦

Rochester, 1984

Rosetta knew she was often sad and tended to over dramatize things, but the years in Rochester had taken their toll. It was like there was a stone tied around her neck and she could not break free. Today things would be different; with Ellen and Martha here there would be plenty of laughs and fun reminiscing about old times.

Larry said he would stop at the grocery and get some of their favorite food: bagels, cream cheese, lox, sable, barbecue chicken and chopped liver. No one made chopped liver like her sister Ellen; she was old enough to learn to make this fresh before Mama died. Rosetta and Martha were too young, but *Mrs. Weinberg* did a pretty good job and would substitute. This was an item Larry's company carried.

Rosetta walked into the living room, growing more excited by the moment. Their plane was due to land at 11:15 am and, if the plane was on time, she would be having lunch with her 2 sisters. They were all that was left. Years ago she had seen her older brother and sister pass away; having to travel to New York to attend the funerals. Harry passed from a second heart attack; ignoring doctors and enjoying life too much to stop smoking and start exercising or dieting. Jessie died in a car accident. While on vacation in Arizona a drunken driver hit her car and the ambulance did not arrive in time.

    Over the years, the family had their share of illness and suffering. Papa and the second wife were now in a nursing home and, according to Ellen and Martha, hardly recognized family members when they visited; often confusing them with nursing staff.

    It was years since she had seen Papa; only visiting when Papa first went into the home. One day Carla forgot she was boiling water and nearly set the apartment on fire. Because of the risk, the City Housing Department said they could no longer keep their subsidized apartment. At first Carla was the one who needed nursing care and Papa being unable to care for Carla went in with her. He would not leave her side; in the home they shared a room and over time Papa began to lose his mental faculties as well.

As Rosetta turned the stations, trying to decide upon the Sunday morning shows, she came upon her favorite preacher. Mr. Billy Silver was running a crusade outside of Memphis and was getting ready to give the keynote sermon. Quickly Rosetta sat down to listen, hoping to pass time before her sisters arrived. O how she loved to watch Mr. Billy; he was tall, handsome and had such marvelous, thick silver-gray hair. It made him look stately and he spoke so eloquently. This was an educated, refined man trying to help people. She did not care that he was not Jewish.

And as Rosetta listened to the music in Mr. Billy's voice, she dozed and traveled back in time, far from her problems.

Chapter II- West 178th Street

Manhattan, New York, 1956

Rosetta helped the boys across the street; she carried Barry, held Jet's hand and Scott trailed behind. Barry was three, Jet nearly six and Scott ten years old. Crossing was never easy, particularly in the middle of the block; cars, buses and trucks high-balled it to get quickly cross-town from the George Washington Bridge to the Harlem River Drive. Or connect with the Washington Bridge at 181st to catch the Major Deegan

Expressway in the Bronx. Most times crossing the street was like playing dodge ball; you really did not want to get hit and close calls were frightening.

Fortunately, Edna's apartment was directly across from their apartment house and Rosetta did not have to carry Barry for long. When safely across, Rosetta put Barry down and held his hand. He was old enough to walk, but easily lost his balance. Seemingly Rosetta rescued Barry from falling on the concrete every couple of minutes. In her other hand, she held Jet who had no trouble walking and Scott closely followed.

Rosetta opened the heavy, glass door to the apartment building and everyone quickly entered before the door closed. As you came into their building, Edna's apartment was the first on the left and Rosetta rang the bell. After two rings she heard Edna call out, "Come in the door is not locked. I left it open for you."

After Edna and Rosetta got the children settled, they sat down in the kitchen to have some coffee and talk. Edna's son and daughter regularly played with the boys. Fred was Scott's age and Carrie was five, nearly six, like Jet. Quickly and naturally, the children began playing. Scott paired with Fred on the hockey game, resuming their tournament; Jet and Carrie played with dolls, making believe they were married, and Barry watched while stacking wooden blocks.

Manhattan, 1956

Rosetta and Edna had been friends for nearly three years and got together a couple of times a week to visit and gossip. Over time they became familiar with the details of each other's lives and enjoyed being together. Sipping coffee Rosetta inquired, "So have you and Mark decided what you are going to do?"

Edna replied, "Not really. The City says it will find us another apartment; according to the Housing Authority it could be any place in Manhattan or the Bronx. They have nearly 1500 families to relocate in Manhattan alone, and when you count up the families in the Bronx, it is a couple of thousand more."

"And the reason for all this again is to make a new highway?"

"Yeah that's what they say; some kind of modern, partially underground road from the George Washington Bridge across the Bronx to connect up with all those different highways. This will speed-up traffic and reduce the time it takes to get cross-town from the George to the eastern Bronx. Eventually in Manhattan there will be apartment buildings, shops, and maybe even a bus terminal built over it. Can you imagine?"

"No not really," Rosetta replied. "How long do they figure this will take?"

"Years. But we have to be out of our apartment in two months."

Rochester, 1984

While Rosetta dozed on her living room sofa, part of her continued recalling their life in Washington Heights, 178th Street and another part listened to Mr. Billy on the television.

"Jesus says, in times of trouble turn toward me. Let Jesus be your strength and salvation. Let him be your safe port in the stormy night. Turn toward Jesus. He is the Light of the World and your Salvation.

When I was a young man and came upon a fork in the road of life, I did not know what to do. My father wanted me to enter the family business and become a farmer; yet there was a voice inside of me that demanded, 'Follow your dreams and listen to your heart.' This was a difficult time and I did not know what to do. Then I remembered the words of the old hymn, 'Turn toward Jesus.' I hit my knees and asked our Lord for an answer, and you all know the rest."

Rochester, 1984

Larry made his first delivery to the Super Shop and, after speaking with the Deli Manager, helped himself to coffee and a cheese danish. Sitting in his car, sipping coffee, Larry thought about their next move.

In a couple of months, he and Rosetta will move back to the City or someplace nearby. This way they can visit the relatives and maybe Rosetta will not be as nervous and sad. Perhaps she will take her heart medicine and care for her health? Nowadays people lived for years after their first heart attack but had to change things about the way they lived.

Perhaps he would reconnect with his sisters. He hadn't spoken to them in years and the emotional distance was really his fault. Faith and Sarah were kind, generous people; as far as Larry could remember, they and their families had always treated everyone with love and respect. Larry realized the distance between himself and his family was due in part to Rosetta's attitude. From the very beginning, they never got along and he never asked, "Why?"

When questioned, Rosetta did not say much, other than she preferred 'her own people.' When Larry brought the boys to visit his parents or sisters, Rosetta stayed home and used the time for herself. After the move to Rochester, it was just easier not to call and further add to the unease around the situation. Sometimes Larry thought Rosetta was stubborn and selfish. He put up with and understand Rosetta did not get along with his family, but her refusal to discuss what happened and what was really going on, was the most frustrating part. Why didn't she let him in? Who knows? He might have understood and even agreed.

Foolishly Larry thought as he got older, things would become less complicated and stressful. Sure, the boys were grown and successfully on their own, except for Barry that is, and needing little from them. The house was sold — they had successfully transitioned to a small apartment and were ready to move on. Yet the two biggest worries in his life, besides Barry were the constraints of not enough money and the implications of Rosetta's worsening health. Early on in their marriage, Rosetta was subject to the 'blues.' Often sitting in their bedroom for hours alone and sad for days. When he asked about it, Rosetta said her mother was the same way; this having started after the birth of the first child.

Larry reasoned Rosetta's dark moods must have something to do with the birthing process; somehow the body's balance must have shifted. Prior to the birth of their first son, Rosetta was happy, full of life and looked forward to going out and being with others. Over the years there were times when she was happy, but it seemed less and less often. When he suggested going to a doctor Rosetta said, "There is nothing the doctors can do. It's heredity. Just like my mother."

Sometimes Rosetta could be so stubborn and justify her own behavior even in the face of medical evidence.

Manhattan, 1956

"Well what are you going to do? Are you going to have the City move you? What does Mark say about all of this?" questioned Rosetta.

Slowly Edna replied, "Mark doesn't know what to do. The move from Wisconsin to New York City has not turned out the way we thought it would. Sure, his company offered more money but it cost more to live here than it does in Milwaukee. Also, Mark and I miss our family. It's early and we still have a few weeks to decide; but we may just pack-up and go back home."

Hesitantly Rosetta offered, "I know you will make the best decision for yourselves, but I hope you stay and get an apartment right around here. If you go, I will miss you."

Manhattan, 1956

After visiting for an hour Rosetta asked Edna to watch Barry and Jet. There was grocery shopping to do and Rosetta liked to have Scott along for company, to learn and carry packages.

Along Broadway, the first place they stopped was the Butcher Shop. As they entered, Scott saw ½ dozen dead chickens hanging upside down in the storefront window. These birds still had their heads, legs and hair, waiting for customers to select them. Depending how the bird was going to be prepared, the Butcher burned off the feathers and quartered, halved or left the bird whole. If desired you kept all the parts of the bird; many customers besides Rosetta enjoyed the feet and entrails, particularly on a freshly killed one.

Today Rosetta wanted *fresh* and went into the back, where the Butcher had the live chickens running around. Scott stood at the doorway and watched Rosetta point out the bird she wanted and the Butcher, after a short chase, captured the chicken, spun it around by its feet to stun and disorient it;

then removed its head on the chopping block. Next, he burnt-off the majority of feathers; usually the customer had to finish the job by hand plucking smaller ones.

Then, he lay the chicken out on the chopping block and cut the bird into quarters; as the bird was opened you could smell its freshness. Scott experienced this many times and liked the heavy musky, sweet odor, knowing this smell insured a fresh, tender bird. Quickly the Butcher wrapped the quarters and entrails with wax paper, then wrapped them again with heavy, brown packing paper.

By this time the Butcher was smiling and complimenting Rosetta; telling her that she picked the healthiest bird and few people still knew how to do this. Usually customers left selection to the Butcher who picked from those pre-killed and hanging in the window. Rosetta replied, her mother taught them all to shop and pick out live poultry. Next, they moved to the front of the store where the Butcher, in his showcase displayed the meats. Today Rosetta needed lamb and veal chops. After looking over what was available, Rosetta made her selection and the Butcher wrapped and packed the meat in a paper shopping bag. Rosetta paid the Butcher who, in-turn, handed the package to Scott to carry.

Leaving the store, Rosetta turned and said, "It's important that you learn how to shop, do laundry and cook. This way, when you are older, you will not have to be dependent upon a woman for these things. It's not good to be dependent upon anyone." Scott replied, "Yes, Mama."

Then, they crossed the street and went into the appetizing store. This store featured a variety of specialty products like herring, lox, chopped liver, sable, pickles and borscht. Arranged in the window and hanging from racks were whole cold cuts like roast beef, bologna, corned beef and aged salamis of various sizes. Today Rosetta needed cold cuts for sandwiches and waited in line. While Rosetta ordered, Scott walked to the pickle barrel, grabbed the tongs and fished for a fresh dill pickle. While he was placing the pickle into a paper wrapper, Rosetta called, "Just one. Daddy gets them for free at his job."

As they left the appetizing store, Scott took a bite of the pickle. It was sour and well-seasoned; almost as good as the pickles his Dad made. Next, they were off to the bakery; this was Scott's favorite store and usually Rosetta let Scott pick out a couple of items. It was up Broadway two blocks by 181$^{St.}$ Street; the short walk gave Scott time to finish the pickle and consider what to buy.

All breads and rolls were freshly baked, as well as the cakes and pastries. Today Scott wanted fresh pumpernickel. Entering the bakery Scott took a number and waited in line; Rosetta watched from outside. When it was Scott's turn, he pointed to a dark bread and called, 'sliced.' After the server cut the bread, in the slicing machine, she placed it in a waxed paper bag and handed it over the counter to Scott. Reaching for the bread, he felt the bread's warmth and softness, having just come out of the oven.

Next Scott ordered a half-portion of seven-layer cake; a chocolate iced cake with seven alternating layers of icing, cream and golden yellow cake filling. Everyone in the family liked this. Scott watched the server cut the piece, then place it on wax paper inside a small cake box, which she then folded and tied up with string. Next the server handed Scott the cake, and he paid for both items.

When Scott walked outside, Rosetta gently questioned him about the cost of each item and amount of change. She wanted to make sure no mistakes were made. When he finished going over price and change, Rosetta smiled and said, "Right again! What do you say, we go across the street and spend this change in Bickfords?"

Happily, both shoppers gathered their packages, crossed the street and walked into Bickford's Cafeteria; Bickford's was a local chain of restaurants that specialized in fast food, cafeteria style, using vending machines. The customer passed through a food line with tray and selected food through vending windows. These were arranged in vertical rows by food type; there was a section for cold and hot plates and another for desserts.

When you saw something you liked, you stopped and placed money in a change slot, then a glass door opened, and you took the dish. Servers worked behind the windows and restocked as items were selected. This was a fun, economical way to buy food and Scott loved their baked beans, which were cooked with a thick, sweetened topping.

Rosetta got herself a coffee and they sat in front of a large plate glass window to watch the shoppers along 181st Street.

Manhattan, 1956

After returning to Edna's apartment, the children were given peanut butter and jelly sandwiches and milk for lunch. When the children were done, Rosetta and Edna made themselves a roast beef sandwich from the fresh cold cuts and bread that were just purchased. At the kitchen table, both slowly bit into their sandwich and smoked a cigarette while they ate. Edna inhaled a *Cool-* menthol while Rosetta puffed away on a *Herbert Tarryton*; a non-filtered brand as strong as *Lucky Strike*.

As the two friends relaxed over sandwiches and smokes, Edna spoke first. "Well did that Butcher, the one who has eyes for you, ask you out again?"

"No thank goodness he didn't. That's why I like to have Scott along with me. It keeps those things to a minimum. While it's flattering to have men tell you how pretty you are as you know right now I have my hands full."

"You're telling me," replied Edna. "Have you decided what you're going to do?" Nervously Edna continued, "You still want me to watch the kids, right? Don't you have to meet Al soon? You know you should meet somewhere beside your apartment. People will talk."

Slowly Rosetta replied. "I know we should go someplace else but it keeps things safe. The apartment is not what you would call romantic. Hopefully nothing will happen with the kids right across the street and Larry due home."

"To tell you the truth, I don't know what I'm going to say. Al and I have been friends for most of our lives. We grew up together and were in the same classes. For years we went our separate ways. Then — out of the blue — he called and wanted to have a cup of coffee for old time sake. I should have said no. I'm a married woman. Who knew he still had feelings for me?"

Edna continued, "It's not right to keep taking gifts from the guy and leading him on. Flirting is one thing but offering hope is another."

Rochester, 1984

While Rosetta dreamed of yesterday, Larry pulled into the parking lot outside *Weegmain's Superstore*. On the route this was the next stop and the newest and most modern supermarket in the area. Larry talked the Beverage Manager into trying some premium root beer and cream soda; this call was a follow-up to see if the product moved. If it sold Larry wanted the manager to carry100 cases each per month in their 10 stores.

Walking from the car to the *Superstore* Larry wondered, "Why am I concerned about this? In a few months we will be living in New York City and it won't matter to me if they carry the product or not. It's not like I get a commission from this sale or even a bonus. I get a flat salary."

As Larry walked toward the store, he realized how much he enjoyed the excitement of the deal and sales. He liked the thrill of the hunt and that's why he was here; sure, he carried a good product, but closing the deal was the real fun and a rush. It felt good to know he still could close the deal.

Somewhere in Time

On tiptoes, as the little girl twirled, she felt the eyes of every person in the audience. All were watching and she sensed how pleased they were with the performance. This was Rosetta's first solo in the spotlight and she smiled and danced on.

In her imagination she was on Broadway, a prima ballerina, dressed in a beautiful costume of white and pink lace. Her ballet shoes were gleaming white and the make-up surrounding her eyes sparkled like evening stars. That night all the fancy men and women had come to see her dance.

And as Rosetta listened to the music, she filled with increased energy and twirled faster. At that moment, she realized in her heart, she was created to dance.

Manhattan, 1956

It started to rain. Al was dressed in a business suit and tried not to get wet walking from the car to Rosetta's building. He still had a few customers left to see and tried to uphold the shining image of fine jewelry salesman. Most customers wouldn't buy from someone sloppily dressed. Right now, Al had other things to consider and was in a hurry, anxious not to be late. "Damn," he silently cursed, "Just my luck to find a parking place three blocks away and it's raining."

As he walked toward Rosetta's building he realized he was nervous and started to rehearse in his mind what he wanted to say. He knew it would be awkward, but he was tired of holding back and dreaming of possibilities, having loved Rosetta since they were children.

Manhattan, 1956

Rosetta sat in the kitchen, watching the cars travel up and down 178th Street, waiting for Al to walk-up the three flights. She had seen his car drive by. For Rosetta there was a hypnotic effect watching the cars, buses and trucks through the open window, and as she focused on their movement, she began to feel calmer.

On the stove she put up a fresh pot of coffee and had some left-over cheesecake, from the weekend, in the refrigerator. This was going to be awkward, but there was little she could do; she had let it get too far.

Manhattan, 1956

Larry left the place early. He told the boss he had a toothache and needed to get to the dentist in Washington Heights before they closed. The boss wondered and questioned why he did not use a local dentist in Brooklyn.

"Won't it hurt driving that far with a sore tooth? Why don't you get it taken care of here? My dentist is two blocks away and I'm sure I can get you in." Larry replied, "It hurts, but sometimes pain is a good thing. It helps clear the mind." The boss just shook his head and replied, "Do what you want. Just be to work on time in the morning." As Larry headed toward the Brooklyn Queens Expressway, he thought, when I'm done today, I won't be the one feeling pain. I'm going to take care of a pain in my ass and he's going to be the one needing dental work."

Manhattan, 1956

By this time Al arrived at Rosetta's apartment and rang the bell. When Rosetta opened the door to let Al in, he leaned forward to kiss Rosetta's cheek but she pulled back; as they walked toward the kitchen she inquired, "I put a pot of coffee on, would you like some? It should be ready." Al replied, "Sure," and as he walked down the hallway and closely observed the apartment, he wondered why they lived this way? He knew Larry did not make much money, but why weren't repairs made to the cracked and broken walls and a fresh coat of paint applied? It certainly would have made the place a little cheerier. Also, in the small five rooms, none of the furniture matched and the whole apartment felt furnished with hand-me-downs.

Yet the children seemed happy, well fed and certainly had enough clothing. When Al questioned Rosetta about the seemingly run-down condition of the apartment, Rosetta smiled and offered, "I'm not much for housekeeping and like an apartment with a lived-in feeling. Also having three sons who are constantly playing, fighting, and fooling around, it's hard to keep up with them. It's not like they have a yard or park where they can run around. They are always breaking something and marking-up the walls." When they had this discussion, Al did not counter and ask, why the boys weren't taught to be less rough or take their energy outside. He knew it was difficult raising children in the City and parents had to be ever-vigilant when their children played outside. Further Al wondered, what type of housekeeper Rosetta would be if they moved in together? Could he get used to this clutter and what about the boys? Was he ready to raise three sons?

When they got settled at the kitchen table Al spoke first. "Rosetta, you look beautiful today. Is that a new dress? Your scarf matches your auburn hair." Rosetta smiled loving the compliment; she liked to dress fashionably, showing off her figure and ever the dancer, liked it when men watched her move.

As Al continued to offer different compliments, nervously Rosetta got up fixed two cups of coffee and took the cheesecake from the refrigerator. She cut them both a slice and after serving, rejoined him at the table. Rosetta was shaking. Having rehearsed this a dozen times in her head, why was she hesitating? She didn't want to hurt Al or perhaps she did not want it to end, enjoying the excitement? Finally, she forced herself to say something.

"Al please stop with the compliments about how good I look. You know I like to hear them but today they are making me nervous." After a few uncomfortable moments of silence, she continued. "We have been friends for most of our lives, haven't we?" Al replied, "Yes we have. It seems like 30 years or more." "Al we can't keep on seeing each other this way. Something has to change."

Taking this as his opportunity Al replied, "I have been thinking the same thing and that's what I came here to discuss." Embarrassed, Rosetta continued. "No Al, I don't think you're following me. It needs to end not go forward."

Somewhere in Time

And as the audience continued to clap their hands and shout out their appreciation, Rosetta joyfully took her bows. When the applause finally died, she scurried from the stage and was met by her smiling mother and father. Effortlessly Ida picked up her daughter and gave her a big kiss on her cheeks, while Poppa called out, "Rosetta you were so beautiful up there and the way you danced made us proud."

In the background, she could see the smiling and envious faces of her brother and three sisters. As Rosetta rested in her mother's arms and Poppa placed his arms around them both, Rosetta hoped; this moment would last forever.

Manhattan, 1956

By this time, Larry's temper cooled, and he circled the block looking for a parking place. He realized in this thing he too played a part; he had known Al for years and until recently Al's relationship with Rosetta had not posed a threat to their marriage. In fact, for the longest time, Larry felt the friendship actually enriched things. When Rosetta excitedly described meeting Al for lunch in the City and his offer to help the boys, through the Pythias Lodge scholarship program go to summer camp, things seemed innocent enough. Also, the friendship served another purpose for Larry; it took some of the financial pressure off him. Going out to lunch gave Rosetta something fun and exciting to do; she enjoyed getting dressed-up and going into the City.

He had known Al for years, and wondered when things got out of hand? Perhaps it was last summer's trip where Al played chauffeur to Rosetta and the family. For one week, they packed up Al's car, the three sisters and six cousins and traveled around the Catskill Mountains. At the last moment, Larry could not take them; he was needed at work when the boss got sick.

Graciously Al stepped in and saved the vacation, to everyone's delight. Perhaps, Larry should have put a stop to things when Al started bringing presents for the kids and Rosetta? Yet Al was a family friend and wanted to do what he could for the family. Besides if he put a stop to things, how would Rosetta react? Al was her friend first.

As Larry parked the car, he figured that Al probably carried feelings for Rosetta for years; the thing kept building and now it was time to end it.

Manhattan, 1956

Turning the corner, Larry saw Al approaching. At first Al wasn't watching, he was walking slowly with eyes cast down. But as they drew closer to each other, Al looked up and caught the cold stare in Larry's eyes. Immediately Al realized it was too early for Larry to get home from work and Larry was coming for him. Al hoped this confrontation would not turn physical, he knew he was no match for Larry's strength; Larry regularly moved 400-pound pickle barrels around and Al barely lifted a suitcase full of jewelry.

As the two rivals drew closer to each other Larry called, "I figured I'd catch you here now. Not man enough to visit when I'm home?" Wanting to avoid a fight, Al considered what to say and before he could decide words jumped out of his mouth. "Why would I come when you're home? You're not the one I want to see."

Startled by this directness Larry replied, "What's that supposed to mean?" Taken aback by the angry tone Al realized he best be cautious. Slowly Al replied, "There were some things I needed to say to Rosetta that's all. These were best said in private."

"Such as?" Larry inquired, wondering how Rosetta had replied.

Al continued walking, and came up to Larry, stopped, looked him directly in the eyes and said, "You're a lucky man," and kept walking past.

Suddenly Larry grabbed Al's shoulder and spun him around. "You know it will be best if you don't come around here anymore. Do you get what I'm saying?"

Continuing on, Larry called, "You don't have to worry about me, I get it."

Manhattan, 1956

When Larry came into the apartment Rosetta was cleaning up the kitchen. At first, she was surprised, then she realized Larry had come home early to catch them. She smiled to herself and thought, "Well Larry you were too late."

Trying to avoid any unpleasantness, Rosetta decided to wait for Larry to bring up the topic. "You're home early," Rosetta inquired, "Would you like something cold to drink?"

"Sure, give me a glass of cold seltzer." As Rosetta got the seltzer from the refrigerator, Larry pressed, "Guess who I ran into downstairs?"

Rosetta figured it was time to be honest. "Larry before you say anything let me talk. A few minutes ago, I told Al that we could no longer be friends. Somehow our friendship, to him, became something more. I told him this was wrong and nothing like that could happen between us. Larry do you understand what I'm saying? Nothing ever happened between Al and me. Over time somehow friendship turned into flirtation, nothing more. I'm sorry if this has caused you heartache."

Slowly tears began to fall from Rosetta's deep, brown eyes and Larry reached to wipe them away. Next, he opened his arms and the two embraced and held each other.

Chapter III- Street Danger

Rochester, 1984

As Rosetta dozed on the living room sofa, the many levels of her mind and consciousness were engaged in activity. Part of her anticipated a visit from her sisters; while another part listened to Mr. Billy on the television. A third part danced in the twilight between worlds; and a fourth continued to solve problems and raise children back on 178th Street.

The wise claim each person is a small universe with hundreds of billions of cells and the energy of our thoughts and feelings has an existence of its own. These thoughts and feelings are always available to be read by those who are correctly attuned. In a small way, each is a reflection of the larger universe, having the potential to create thought and regulate, through the life force, our own body and physical environment.

Further when we look-up at the night sky and see the light from a distant world, this light is billions of years old. In effect, we are observing the lives of beings who lived and died eons ago. When this light finally reaches us, it is filled with the collective energy of their thoughts, hopes and desires and on an inner level, if aligned, we are able to connect with their existence. On this higher, inner level there is no time and distance, and through the Light and our energy, we are all connected.

As Rosetta continued to project her thoughts and feelings, we the receivers of this energy, participate in her experience and also benefit.

Rochester, 1984

Finally, Larry tracked the Manager down; he was in the back storeroom supervising the unloading of a truck. The Manager wanted to make sure that he received the correct amount of product before signing and releasing the driver.

As Larry walked into the Manager's field of sight, Larry called out, "Hey Joey why are you breaking this guy's balls? Can't your Foreman make sure the pallets are accurate? You have to do this yourself?"

Recognizing Larry's voice and not looking up from his count Joey replied, "This is what I should have done with your delivery; had my Foreman check it so I wouldn't have gotten upset. Seems we were light 6 cases. Larry you wouldn't know anything about that would you?"

By this time Joey was smiling and walking toward Larry. Joey turned the rest of the job over to his Foreman who was finishing up the count on a delivery of lettuce. As they drew closer to each other, Larry reached out and shook Joey's hand, "So my delivery was short was it? I sent my best man; he hasn't been short in 5 years. I smell a rat. I think you know more about this than you are saying."

By now they were both laughing and walking toward the lounge in the front of the warehouse. After they got themselves a cup of coffee, they found chairs and sat down.

"So, are you still planning to pack-up and move back to the City?" Joey inquired. "Why do you ask?" Larry replied.

"Well I was just getting used to your ugly face and don't want to have to deal with anyone else. Those sodas you had us try moved in two days and customers came back wanting more. What's in those bottles, something addictive?"

"No there's nothing addictive in them. They use only the highest-grade ingredients. It's the best line of soda I've tasted in years."

"Me too. Listen I spoke to the bosses and we want to start with 100 cases per month in this store. If it moves, in two months, we will increase the order for all 10 of our stores in this area. Then if it goes like I think it will, we raise the order for all thirty stores. What do you think?"

Larry smiled and extended his hand. "You want 100 cases each for the cream and root beer, right?" Joey smiled and said, "That's what I like about you, always pushing."

"Well, I want to make sure I get the order right?"

"OK, 100 cases each."

Manhattan, 1956

While Edna and Rosetta sat outside on the highest step leading into the Synagogue talking, Carrie, Jet and Barry played house sitting on the sidewalk in front of the large building. Carrie brought along her baby carriage and dolls; Jet played the role of adoring husband, while Barry was oldest child and brother to baby-dolls Jeanine and Francine.

Around the corner, about 30 feet away Fred and Scott played box-ball; a street version of tennis, using your hands as rackets with dividing lines in the sidewalk, concrete as net and boundary. As usual Scott was winning, and John was complaining about his poor luck.

"Well how did you *make-out* with Al?" inquired Edna. With that choice of words Rosetta shot Edna a look that could kill.

"Sorry about the phrasing, but you know what I mean; the other day how did things work out between you and Al?" said Edna.

"Actually, they worked out pretty well. Although it was kind of sad. I think Al was going to ask me to leave Larry and really didn't expect me to end it, you know."

Hesitating, Edna dug for more dirt. "What really went on between you and Al? You can tell me I won't tell a soul; not even Mark."

"Nothing ever happened between us. We were always friends; just a friendly kiss on the cheek, a hug, nothing more. Somehow over time Al became more and more a part of our lives; helping with this and that. Giving the kids birthday presents and taking me out to lunch, giving jewelry. At first, I didn't think anything about it; you know he is a jewelry salesman. But I guess I enjoyed the attention and excitement of the flirtation. Now I can never see Al again."

"What did Larry say to all of this? You did tell him, didn't you?"

"Well by now, I'm sure a lot of people saw them together on the street, overheard their angry words and spread the story all over. Larry figured out something was going on and came home early to end it."

"They ran into each other on the street. This occurred after I had told Al that we could not be friends or anything else. He was very upset and said he would miss me. I said I would miss him as a friend and should not have let the relationship develop the way it did."

"Larry was pretty angry and said he should have seen this thing coming and not taken advantage of Al's generosity. Hopefully this thing is in the past. I sure hope so. Emotionally it has taken a lot out of me."

Somewhere in Time

As the little ballerina rested in her bedroom smiling and recreating in her mind the evening's dance performance, she heard a knock. "Rosetta dear can we come in?" It was Rosetta's mother, Ida who spoke. Slowly Rosetta replied, "Come in."

Ida and Louie, Rosetta's parents entered. It was Louie who everyone called Poppa who spoke next. "Rosetta we are so proud of the way you danced tonight; like a gazelle you floated across the stage. Your mother and I were talking and decided not to wait; we have a special present that we were waiting to give on your 13th birthday." Rosetta exclaimed, "A present for me! What did you get?"

Slowly Poppa reached into his pocket and pulled out a ball of white tissue paper. As he opened the paper he spoke, "Sorry we did not get the present wrapped," as I said, "We decided not to wait."

Then he held before Rosetta a brilliant gold Star of David, clasped on a finely fashioned gold chain. Ida remarked, "This piece was my mother's and she wanted you to have it. She too was a dancer and said to me, whichever of your children dances and reaches for the stars, give this to him or her."

As Poppa put the necklace around Rosetta's neck, Ida continued "Traditionally the Star of David is also called Solomon's Seal, the six-pointed star representing the power of the great King himself. Some people claim this symbol is even older; the coming together of the two triangles that form the star being the point at which heaven met the earth. Did you know there is a constellation in this form? Enough with legends and traditions, tonight it has another meaning. Here in this room one star greets another."

Happily, Rosetta held the fine gold in her hand and examined the exquisite piece slowly in the mirror; was it her imagination or did she feel the metal begin to grow warm? Yes, it was growing warmer and there was a loving, peaceful energy emanating from it. Rosetta smiled and bathed in this light as the two stars became one.

Rochester, 1984

Joey finished and he asked Larry to go for a walk through the warehouse. He said, there was something he wanted Larry to see. As they distanced themselves from the other employees who were on break, Joey continued. "Larry you really know your stuff; whenever you recommend a product or offer a suggestion about the warehouse, you're right on. We could use someone like you at *Weegmaine's*."

Somewhat surprised Larry replied, "Joey you're offering me a job? You want me to work for you. Where did this come from?"

"Not so loud. That's why I asked you go for a walk to get away from the others; if they heard this, they would really be pissed."

"Joey what's the deal? The job here isn't big enough for two Managers; how does this figure?"

"Well they're bumping me up and the bosses asked for a recommendation on who I thought could do the job? I really don't have anyone working with me who I think can move this section forward. You have the right kind of attitude and love the sales game. Well what do you think? I'm sure the money will be more than you're making and its close to home."

"Joey, Joey what can I say? You know we were thinking about moving back to the City. I just don't know. Rosetta was looking forward to living near her family again."

"Look you don't have to decide today. Give it a few days. Talk it over with Rosetta. After you have this under your belt and do the job I know you can do, who knows what can happen? The Company is planning an expansion and moving down state. Maybe they will relocate you? Even if you only do it for a year or two think of the money you can put away for your move."

Rochester, 1984

After working out some of the details with Joey, Larry sat in the car and considered what to do. Should he call Rosetta and discuss this opportunity on the phone, or should he continue along with his route and wait until the end of the day? Later after supper would be the best time. He could not barge in in the middle of the day; it had to come across as if he were not even interested. He had given his word and Rosetta badly wanted to be near her family.

"Shit," Larry cursed to himself. "For so many frigging years, working for a boss that barely paid enough to make the bills, let alone go on vacation. Now here was a golden opportunity placed right in my lap and we're packed ready to move. Promises were made; I can't go back on my word. Or could I? No, it had to come across that this was Rosetta's idea because financially it was best to delay the move."

Having decided upon a strategy, Larry turned on the ignition, put the car in drive and headed out toward Gates. This was one of the distant suburbs and there was an appetizing store that carried their line of products.

Manhattan, 1956

Finishing up a cigarette and wanting to change the subject, Rosetta inquired, "Well you've heard about my problems. Now what's going on with you? Have you guys decided what you're going to do? Are you going back to Milwaukee or will you keep it going here?"

Slowly Edna replied, "We're not sticking it out. By the end of August, we're leaving for Milwaukee; we don't want the kids to miss much school. School starts earlier in Wisconsin. I know that's not what you were hoping."

Quietly Rosetta nodded her head and listened; all the while she felt a dull pain in her heart. Rosetta's worst fear had been realized; Edna was like another sister, someone whom Rosetta could tell everything without fear of being judged. Not like many others and their 'higher than mighty' attitude of knowing what was best.

"We both agree New York City is not what we thought it would be," continued Edna. "We thought the City would be filled with glamour and excitement. We thought, every week we would go out and see Broadway Shows. It's nothing like that. We cannot afford that life. Actually, there were more things for the family to do in Wisconsin and we never had to pay a baby-sitter."

"My mother says we can move in with her, until we get settled and find a place of our own. I started the job of packing and we will tell the kids in a couple of days. Mark has given notice and requested that he be reinstated in his old job. Fortunately, there might be an opening soon."

With difficulty Rosetta spoke softly so the kids would not hear. "Jeez, Edna. I will miss you guys. Also, I feel terrible that things did not work out for you. You know whenever Larry comes up with an idea about moving out of the City and trying something new, I'm afraid something bad will happen and it all will fall apart."

Edna looked at her friend and offered, "We both made the decision and wanted to live in the big City; if we never came here to live we would have missed this experience and I never would have met you. You see in the process good things happened."

As the two friends continued to console each other, Fred and Scott were thirsty and came around the corner of the building to ask for a cold drink. Just as they approached, Scott heard a crackling noise from overhead. Carrie, Jet and Barry were still seated on the sidewalk having a cup of imaginary tea. Instantly, Scott looked up and before he could say a word, one of the large flag poles that hung horizontally over the steps broke away from its support. This heavy 30-foot wooden pole fell straight down, and landed with a thud, bounced back-up and fell back down again, missing Barry and the doll stroller by inches.

Fortunately, Carrie and Jet were seated a few feet away on the far side of the stroller and were also physically unaffected by the falling pole. Frightened Barry began to cry, having been startled by being so close to getting hurt. Then Carrie and Jet started crying, joining Barry with their tears.

By now Rosetta and Edna rushed down the steps and quickly moved their children away from the fallen flagpole; the entire time watching its twin, to see if it was coming undone. As they sheltered their children and moved them out of harm's way, the custodian of the Synagogue came rushing out calling, "I heard the loud, crashing noise, was anyone injured?"

Rosetta called out to him, "My youngest son missed being crushed and killed by inches. Don't you people check these things? This is a busy street; it could have fallen on anyone. You need to be more careful, a house of God and all!"

The custodian replied, "We painted last week, and they were sturdy enough. Let me get my ladder and check the other pole. I'm sorry. Are you sure everyone is uninjured? I don't know what else to say."

By this time, everyone was walking quickly toward Edna's apartment trying to get as far away from the danger zone as possible.

Rochester, 1984

For a moment Rosetta opened her eyes and massaged her temples. She thought to herself, this headache would not quit. Then she stared at the clock on top of the television set and counted how long until her sisters arrived. Yes, time was moving slowly and it was only 10 minutes into Mr. Billy's program. As Rosetta was now almost awake, trying her best to forget her aches and pains, she focused her attention back on Mr. Billy's words.

"Each of us is weak and this weakness helps us turn to that which is strong. Jesus says, if you take one step toward me, I will take 10 steps toward you.

Who among us does not need Jesus? Who among us is without sin?"

As Mr. Billy posed this question, Rosetta had to smile. Yes, Mr. Billy it was only 2 years ago that you were found with your pants down, in your sports car, with a young lady who was completely butt-naked. Considering this lady was not your wife, there was some explaining to do. Yet in time we forgave you. In fact, to me this momentary weakness made you more real. For who among us has not done something they would rather forget?

And as Mr. Billy continued to talk on Rosetta wondered about sin. In their Faith, 10 Commandments traditionally were used to identify sinful or bad behaviors and if broken, there was literally 'hell to pay.'

However, Rosetta often found herself wondering about other behaviors like selfishness. Being a mother required all of her time and she wished she had some time for herself to dance, and just do things she loved to do as a woman, not just a mother. In some people's view, that took away from their kids. Yet if she gave and gave, in time there would be nothing left of herself. Thinking of oneself instead of another, sometimes was a survival necessity. So how far could you go with what you wanted before it was too much?

And as Rosetta considered this weighty question, it was enough for her to close her eyes and push her back to sleep. And as Mr. Billy talked about the virtues of personal redemption and Holy Forgiveness, Rosetta dozed off once again.

Chapter IV- School Days

Manhattan, 1956

It was early October and the City streets cooled from the summer's heat, getting ready for their rush into winter's cold. The children had gone back to school and Edna's family returned to Wisconsin. With the change of season and the start of school, there was little time to mourn the loss of friendship or think about and watch the new highway construction around them.

With the closing of stores, shopping patterns had to change, and school clothing and supplies purchased had to be found elsewhere. Errands that took minutes to complete, now were extended and over the last month farewells were offered to people who owned and worked in the local fruit store, Woolworth Department Store, Buster Brown Shoe Store, local shoemaker, a jeweler and children's clothing store.

Slowly each of the local stores, in a two-block radius stretching nearly 2 miles across Manhattan had going out of business sales and were eventually boarded-up. The many tenement buildings that filled the condemned area and were home to thousands of people, over the months closed and were vacated.

Gradually 10 feet high wooden walls were constructed to box-in and protect the construction area. Then the bulldozers and wrecking balls went to work. In a matter of weeks, where there once stood fine churches, synagogues, liquor stores, bars, tenement buildings, and retail stores, all vanished into a cloud of dust and fallen bricks.

The local resident insect and rodent population also now needed other places to live, and when they realized what was happening around them, quickly moved across the street into the surviving apartment buildings. For months, residents turned on the lights in the kitchen long before they entered and the local hardware stores could not stock enough mousetraps and roach spray.

Now when children played in the street and local alleyways, they joked with each other about how many new pets they had. Less mirthful were the stories about lying in bed and feeling the roaches fall from the walls and ceiling into bed with you. Brushing roaches off your face and head bothered even the toughest among them. Also many were the tales of seeing shadows dart across the floor and having a funeral 'for Mickey Mouse' outside the incinerator room.

And as the City and State worked to upgrade the transportation system for millions of travelers, long before the first toll booth was erected on the new road, others paid dearly for this progress.

Manhattan, 1956

To get Jet and Scott safely to school daily, Poppa Louie traveled from his apartment in the Bronx and walked with them the seven blocks. Neither was old enough to wait for the traffic lights and cross the busy Manhattan Streets alone, particularly Broadway near 173rd Street. The talk at the schoolyard, among the young students who could not cross alone, was a different story about a person not being careful enough. The worst stories involved a City bus. Usually they had to scrape what was left of the person off the pavement.

Each day when school ended, when Poppa Louie was not available, Rosetta picked up the boys. While Jet was in kindergarten, she had to make the trip twice daily. Jet got out at 12:00 and Scott 3:00 pm. Usually in the warm weather, like today she brought a lunch for everyone. From the school, they ate across the street in Washington Park. Sometimes Rosetta stayed until Scott got out of school watching Jet and Barry play.

It was on days like this, when the boys were playing and she was watching them dash about filled with youthful energy, Rosetta felt most alive. Tending to the little ones, as they reached upward toward the sun and their future dreams, connected Rosetta with the rhythm of life. She was moving in tune with the grand dance and lost herself in the music of tending to others.

Manhattan, 1956

This was one of those rare October days where summer makes a short reappearance; it is traditionally known as Indian Summer and as the sun rose higher in the sky so did the temperature. Fortunately for the boys Rosetta brought their swimsuits to the park, and with a little cooperation there was a way for them to cool off. As the mothers sat around and talked, watching their children play and grow warmer, one of the ladies sought out the Park Supervisor.

On behalf of the other ladies and their children, she went to request that the wading pond sprinkler spray be turned on for one more afternoon. This spray which was set in the center of a large concrete circle with drain, and was affectionately named the wading pond, was turned-off for the season the day after Labor Day. With some verbal flattery or a donation of food the Park Supervisor could be persuaded to let the water run. In reality it was not that difficult of a task and involved going into the mechanical building and resetting the valve. The Supervisor who enjoyed watching the children play in the water and had a youngster of his own generally did not put up that big an argument.

Rosetta brought Barry to the park in his stroller and packed lunches for everyone. Knowing the day would become hotter as it progressed, Rosetta planned to spend the entire afternoon in the park. When Scott got out of school at 3:00 pm he could play for a while in the spray, then they would all go home for supper.

Getting up early, Rosetta prepared chicken with carrots and potatoes for dinner and needed to reheat the dish in the oven for 20 minutes or so when they got home. This short period was not enough time to get the rest of the apartment hot and she did not have to keep the hungry boys waiting long. Usually when Larry got home later in the evening, Rosetta sat down and ate with him. After the long 1 ½ hour commute from Brooklyn, Larry liked to relax and eat slowly; this was never possible with three boys talking, complaining, and hitting each other. Over the years, it was just easier to have two sittings for dinner.

When Scott got out of school, he crossed the street with the assistance of a crossing guard and ran into the park to find his mother and brothers. Washington Park is located directly across the street from Public School 173 and is a full park with playground, wading pond, softball field, handball courts and open fields. As Scott grew older, he enjoyed playing the different games and sports. Today he brought to school a softball glove and wanted to see if he could get involved in a pick-up game with some of the older boys. After Scott had a glass of cool-aid and chocolate chip cookies that Rosetta packed, he ran off to the dirt ball field in order to get picked by one of the teams. Usually he was picked someplace in the middle and was recognized as being a good player by the older boys.

With Scott running off to play softball, Rosetta brought Jet and Barry to the women's bathroom. She carried Barry while Jet trailed behind, and quickly found a vacant stall to change the boys into their swimsuits. She packed their clothes in her carryall as they left the bathroom excitedly walking toward the wading pool.

Jet wasted no time and ran into the pool; his feet were protected by plastic swimming shoes and he quickly made his way through the water which was 2 inches deep to the spray itself. Barry was shyer and Rosetta had to encourage him to get wet. She stayed behind the black rod iron fence that encircled the pond, holding Barry's hand as he sat on the perimeter wall of the circle. This wall was six inches high and he was content to rest and splash his feet in the cool water.

As Rosetta watched Jet play with the water and tease the others, as it came out of the large spray head, she smiled at his boldness. Feeling the cool, spray mist as it traveled on the breeze and caressed her face, Rosetta relaxed. The warm, October sun was at her back, her children were playing, and Rosetta mused about her boy's different temperaments. They seemed to be born with a uniqueness each their own. Each was subject, within varying amounts to the same opportunity and restrictions. Yet each was different and wanted different things from life. Jet was curious and adventurous, easily getting into trouble and joyful of evoking responses from others. Scott was introspective and seemed to enjoy being alone. Barry was fearful and stubborn; easily frustrated, losing his temper when things didn't work out for him.

She worried the most about Barry; in her mind he was the most fragile of the three. When she tried to discuss her fears with Larry, he dismissed her concern saying, "He's only three years old. He has plenty of time to outgrow this stubbornness and fear." Rosetta did not agree and said, "There's something there; I'm telling you."

Then Barry stood, carried his water pail and began walking into the water; he bent over and splashed himself and jumped up and down. He was laughing and enjoying the warm sun and cool water. He turned to Rosetta and called, "Look at me, Mommy!" Rosetta smiled and waved, "Yes, you're a big boy." Again, Barry laughed and joined some of the other children who were playing with their buckets and water toys. He too began to fill up his water bucket.

And as Rosetta watched Barry enjoy himself, she breathed a sigh of relief. Perhaps she was being overly concerned and melodramatic? Who knew how one's life would develop? Then Rosetta took a deep breath and breathed in the fresh October air and found a seat on a nearby bench so she could watch her children play in the water.

Manhattan, 1956

When she got the boys home, Rosetta told Scott to stay downstairs and play while she got dinner ready and bathed Jet and Barry. Scott took his glove and ball and went into the alley between the tenement buildings. Often, he tossed a rubber ball against the building and practiced fielding and throwing for hours. Or if other kids were around, they would play a game of punch ball; this was a street version of baseball without bats and no pitching. When it was your turn to bat, you bounced the ball and punched it with your fist. You got two chances at punching the ball; then you ran to the bases before the other team threw you out by hitting you with the ball.

Today the other children were upstairs getting ready for dinner, so Scott practiced his fielding by throwing grounders against the building wall. All around the alley, the other buildings served as a boundary, so Scott didn't have to run far when he missed. Also, their apartment windows on the third floor overlooked the alley, and Rosetta called down whenever she needed one of them.

As it was a warm day, all of the windows to their apartment were wide open. The kitchen window opened to a small 2-foot platform for plants and food storage in the winter. Suddenly something told Scott to turn around and look-up at the windows to their apartment. When he turned, hoping to see Rosetta calling him upstairs, Scott was stunned. For some reason, Barry was trying to climb out the kitchen window; he was struggling to pull himself up onto the window ledge. Slowly he pulled himself up and crawled out the window onto the small wooden plant platform.

Scott was horrified. In a matter of seconds if something wasn't done, Barry would tumble three stories to his death. Then Scott began to yell, "Barry! Stop and go back into the kitchen! Barry! Stop! Now!" Hearing Scott shout his name, Barry froze for an instant.

Then, miraculously, Rosetta appeared at the window and pulled Barry to safety.

Somewhere in Time

Playfully Rosetta grabbed Martha's hand and urged, "Pretend you're the man this time. It's your turn to lead." Then the two sisters twirled and swayed to the music on the radio. As the music began to play faster, Rosetta increased her tempo and gradually lost herself in the notes; while part of her followed her sister's lead, another part was set free, moving to the melody and dancing free, far from her life on Undercliff Avenue, Bronx, New York.

In those rare moments, when Rosetta focused on the notes, moved with their intensity and became one with them, she and the music existed together, apart from everything else. And as she soared, twirled and danced in another reality, Martha interrupted. "Rosetta, are you getting nervous about your tryouts for the City Dance

Program? I know you have been practicing daily."

For a brief moment, Rosetta was called back from the joyous world of motion where she existed apart from daily care and offered. "If I do not make it into the advanced program, I will be very disappointed. I feel alive when I am moving to the music and feeling it vibrate through my body."

Like a good sister, Martha replied, "I know you will make it. You're the best dancer anyone around here has seen."

Rochester, 1984

As Larry drove north toward the town of Gates, he chuckled to himself and spoke out loud. "Sometimes life is a bitch. When it rears its head and plays a joke on you, all you can do is laugh." And Larry continued to laugh.

Gradually he pulled into the middle lane and cruised at the speed limit so he could use the time to think. Many were the day when he wished he had a job like the one that was just offered. The extra money would make so many things easier and possible, and the excitement of working in a growing company where his skills were highly valued, had been something only to dream about.

Where he presently worked, the owners really didn't want anyone with new ideas or who could think too much. They wanted to do the planning, make the big decisions and a Foreman to carry them out. Early on, Larry realized when either of the owners asked for an opinion, they really wanted someone to agree with them. At first, Larry found this hard to do but as time wore on, he recognized, beneath their sarcasm and embarrassed looks, what was going on.

The first couple of planning sessions, when he pointed out the limitations in a selling strategy or a logistical problem neither considered, Larry saw the look of resentment in their eyes. Quickly he understood, unless a decision was being made that would immediately sink the business, his job was to agree. He never forgot when the Principal Owner laughed and teased, "You know Larry, if you are so smart perhaps you should go out on your own and show us how to do it."

As Larry focused on the highway, he started to feel good about himself. It was a compliment at his age being offered such a big and important job — Regional Beverage Manager. Usually as you got older and got closer to social security, bosses figured your mind stopped working. Yet Larry never felt sharper; he saw things more clearly and was able to concentrate with less mental energy wasted worrying about making mistakes. Because of his experience, Larry rarely made them.

Too bad he made the promise to Rosetta to move back to the City. What would it take to get her to change her mind? He wondered. If he took this job, there would be plenty of money and they could travel more. Yet these last couple of years Rosetta had not been well. Could this disappointment be too much for her?

Manhattan, 1956

Rosetta pulled Barry into the kitchen and nervously hugged him to her breast. Angrily she scolded, "Barry what were you doing out there? I told you to sit in the living room until I called you to join Jet in the bathtub. Why didn't you listen to me?"

Then Barry began to cry and stammered between his tears, "Mommy, Mommy I was looking for you. I thought you left me. I was looking for you."

"You could have fallen. I was in the bathroom not outside the window. Never, never do that again"

"OK Mommy. OK Mommy."

Manhattan, 1956

Later as each of the three boys finished-up their bath and played in Jet and Barry's room, Rosetta had a few moments alone before dinner with her thoughts. She sat in her bedroom, smoked a cigarette and gazed at the late afternoon sunshine as it reflected off the apartment windows of the buildings across the alley.

"Today we were lucky again," she thought, "A few seconds later and Barry would have been gone. In life sometimes all it took was a matter of seconds. Barry, Barry, sometimes I think you will be the death of me. This was the second time I almost lost you. O Barry I love you so much. When Larry gets home, I will make him get a hold of the building Superintendent and put bars across the window. I can't take a chance like that again."

"Thank God for mother's intuition. Something told me to leave Jet while he played with his bath toys and get Barry ready. Just as I was walking toward the living room, I heard Scott yelling. Fortunately, I reached Barry in time."

And as Rosetta puffed on her cigarette, she heard soft violin music coming from the alley below. As the notes gently drifted-upward, Rosetta stood and looked outside the bedroom window and saw, standing in the alley a traveling gypsy violinist. He was colorfully dressed in traditional costume and accompanied by a young girl, in a white and brown dress, who danced along to the music. And as the violin music filled the alley with a sad, mournful tune of lost opportunity and love, other apartment dwellers stood at their windows to listen and watch the performers.

Quickly Rosetta went into the kitchen, got some change from her purse and wrapped it in a tissue. Then, she walked back into the bedroom, opened the window and tossed the change to the performers below.

And as the mournful, violin music continued and the young dancer interpreted the tune, Rosetta grew sadder. Gradually, a tear fell from her eye and she sobbed along with the music, crying for everything she had given-up in her life. Then as the music continued, she wondered, why she had given-up dance? So long ago, it had meant so much to her.

Chapter V- Rosetta's Blues

Somewhere in Time

Rosetta had been in bed for four days. She and Martha shared the room together and Martha had done and said everything she could to help cheer-up her sister. Rosetta's parents were growing worried, in their time they had seen every possible childhood illness, however this was a new problem for them.

Dr. Melvin called it melancholia or the blues. When he diagnosed the problem, Ida, Rosetta's mother recognized having similar symptoms after the birth of their first child. In time these symptoms passed and 'in the old country' this was a common occurrence. Something about the hormones changing in childbirth. Yet what did a 12-year-old girl have to be this sad about?

Finally, after a week of lying in bed and being unable to get-up and resume normal activity, Rosetta began to cry uncontrollably for hours at a time. This crying and loss of appetite worried everyone. Dr. Melvin prescribed a light sedative to calm Rosetta's nerves and urged the family to be patient. When Rosetta was ready, Dr. Melvin said, she would talk about what was bothering her. The other alternative, putting Rosetta in a hospital, at her young age, was not something to be undertaken lightly.

During the early part of the second week, while her brother and sisters were at school, Rosetta began to sob and called for her mother. "Mama, Mama, I need you. I am so ashamed. I am so ashamed."

Hearing Rosetta call, Ida rushed into the bedroom. "Rosetta, Rosetta dear, what is it? What are you so ashamed about? Take your time and tell me."

Sobbing Rosetta said, "I'm ashamed of them. I'm ashamed of them."

Not understanding, Ida gently questioned, "Please honey, I'm not following you. What are you ashamed about? You know you can trust me."

With an embarrassed voice, "My breasts. My breasts. They are too big. They are too big. At dance class, the other dancers were making fun of me. They were making fun and said I couldn't be a dancer. Professional dancers were flat chested. O Mama is it true? Is it true? Are they too big for me to become a dancer?"

Lovingly Ida leaned over the bed and hugged her daughter. Softly she rubbed her back and spoke. "Rosetta you are growing into a beautiful, full-figured woman. Many women will be envious of your form and beauty. They will try to hurt you and you must be careful of their jealousy."

Realizing that her question was not answered, Rosetta persisted. "Mama is it true? Are professional dancers 'small' in that area?"

Not wanting to further hurt her daughter and not wishing to be untruthful, Ida paused then answered. "For the most part that is true. There are many dance forms that require a slim build. Yet I do not know everything. Perhaps there are some forms that allow for full proportions."

Hearing this from her mother, Rosetta turned away, lay face down on the bed and began to cry again. All the while, Ida rubbed her daughter's back and repeated, "Perhaps God has something else in store for you Rosetta? You do not know. You have to have faith. Perhaps your figure will make a man happy and will help raise young children? Rosetta you have to be strong."

Somewhere in Time

Finally, Rosetta stopped crying and fell asleep. Quietly Ida stood and tiptoed out of the bedroom. As she walked out of the room, Rosetta's deep breaths were interspersed with an occasional sob. Ida thought, "Dreams die hard. Most times we do not understand what fate has in store for us and we must learn not to fight so hard. Sometimes fighting against our destiny makes it that much more difficult."

While Rosetta slept, she dreamed and in her dream she found much comfort. In her dream, she saw a girl, lying in bed, recovering from something. This young girl was in a room that was part of a larger house, a rehabilitation hospital of sorts. Yet it was unlike modern facilities for all the walls and floors were of glass and you could see through them into the different rooms.

And as the young girl rested for days in bed, she grew healthier and drew strength and comfort from the next room. For in the center of the next room was a gray, unmarked, rectangular box. This was a mysterious box; for it never opened yet pulsated with a loving, gentle energy that reached out and perpetually caressed Rosetta. Daily from inside this box, this energy changed, entertaining Rosetta with the story of different lives which she lived. In each of these changing stories, which were varied, rich and full of adventure, Rosetta continued to bathe in love and peace. In her dream, Rosetta was content to stay in this place of many opportunities and spiritual healing forever.

Somewhere in Time

Finally one morning, when Rosetta awoke, she was renewed. Happily she got out of bed and walked over to her chest-of-drawers in the corner of the room. Quickly she changed out of her nightclothes and selected clothing for the outdoors. Then without thinking removed her cherished Star-of-David and placed it in the gray metal jewelry box in the bottom drawer.

Then Rosetta called out. "Mama. Mama, I am better. Today I am better. What's for breakfast?"

Rochester, 1984

Larry was hungry and pulled into the Gates Diner where they served breakfast 24 hours a day. Having just been offered the job of a lifetime, Larry figured he would celebrate with some eggs and home fries.

As he waited for his order, he fought the impulse to call Rosetta and tell her about the job offer. She was hard to figure and changeable; sometimes generous, loving and kind. Other times when the blues hit, she was mean spirited and controlling. It was like there were two women in the same body. As he sipped the hot, steaming coffee he decided to stay with his initial reaction. Wait until tonight after the sisters were settled in and discuss the possibilities and problems in person.

While Rosetta was unpredictable, Larry never regretted marrying and sharing his life. From the moment they met he was head-over-heels in love and did everything he could to make her happy. Rosetta was a striking beauty with long auburn hair, deep, brown eyes, soft, blemish-free skin and a trim, full-figure. When they were dancing, Larry saw the envy in the eyes of the other men and could sense jealousy in the hearts of other women.

They had gotten married young, before Larry had a chance to separate from the Navy and set-up in business. The War was on, it was uncertain times and everyone was in a rush. Looking back, it would have made more sense to wait, however, he was afraid if they waited, he might lose her.

Not everyone could boast they married a Rockette. More accurately, someone who auditioned for the famous Radio City female dance troop. Certainly, Rosetta was a beauty and when she danced, there was electricity in the air. When Larry questioned Rosetta about her try-out, she grew defensive and quickly stated, "It was not for me."

Over time, Larry learned from Ida that Rosetta easily passed the glamour and beauty portion of the audition but lacked the necessary technical ability. According to the producer, Rosetta had good basic skill but not the more advanced level required. To him, it appeared she gave-up learning at a point and missed the opportunity to practice and develop further. The producer told Rosetta to practice and come back when she was ready.

Then Larry and the War came along. Somehow Rosetta never got around to taking advanced dance classes and practicing. When Rosetta was in a bad mood, she used to blame Larry for getting in the way of her dancing career and stopping her from being on stage. Now she just blamed him for dragging her off to Rochester and losing his good paying job which had brought them here.

It wasn't always like this. In her more reasonable moments, Rosetta recognized her part in how their lives turned out. Usually she was not shy or afraid to state her mind.

In recent years, she had become apologetic about not encouraging Larry's different business ventures where he wanted to go out on his own. Rosetta had been the one who was fearful about risks and taking a chance. Also, she had resisted moving out of the City many times; in fact, twice Larry put down payments on homes in the suburbs and Rosetta refused to move.

Slowly she had come to understand she was as responsible as he was for their limited financial resources. Now with the latest job offer all of this could finally change.

Rochester, 1984

Suddenly Rosetta shook herself awake. Mr. Billy finished his sermon and now there was a Christian Rock Band playing their version of "Amazing Grace" on the tube. Perhaps it was the change to music that stirred her? Again, Rosetta looked at the clock; it was only 11:30 am. She mumbled, "Boy time sure flies when you're having fun."

Rosetta shook off the dull pain in her head and walked from the living room to the small, dining area. These rooms merged into each other and Rosetta stood by the window watching the back parking lot. In some magical way, she reasoned if she looked out the window long enough, eventually Larry would pull-in with Ellen and Martha.

Part of her understood that the plane was not due to land for another 15 minutes. Yet she reasoned, in her life, stranger things had happened.

And as Rosetta lit another smoke, inhaling deeply, she wondered why she liked Mr. Billy and some of the other Sunday morning preachers. Most of them were con artists just out to make an easy buck. Yet what if one of them was honest and actually found something of value in their religion? That would be something Rosetta wanted to know about; it had been a very long time since she had something to believe in other than disappointment and heartache.

Come on Rosetta, she reminded herself, your life has not been that bad. Here you go again forever the drama queen. We all know, no one's life has been as bad as your life. And Rosetta laughed at her own joke. Lately it seemed the best conversations she had were with herself.

Looking out the window, Rosetta took comfort that soon Ellen and Martha would be sitting at this dining room table having a cup of coffee. It would be like old times, in Washington Heights, when they visited each other weekly. Sometimes two and three times a week. In those years, Rosetta spoke easily with her sisters and confided many things.

Rochester, 1984

Feeling dizzy from the cigarette, Rosetta held onto a nearby chair and gradually sat down. Her head began to spin and she thought, "Boy I had better give these damn things up; for sure they will be the death of me."

And as Rosetta sat on one of the dining room chairs, that faced the window that overlooked the back parking lot, she slowly fell back to sleep and dreamed about her life on 178th Street. Part of her consciousness was searching for something she had lost many years ago.

Manhattan, 1956

"You mean you're not going to allow him to have the shots? What's the matter with you both? At the very least, let Hal take another look at him; he's got doctor friends that he went to school with at the Public Health Department and can call them for advice," questioned Ellen. Incredulously both Ellen and Martha could not believe what they were hearing.

Tentatively Rosetta replied, "They say, if symptoms are going to develop, it takes about three days. This is the end of the second day and so far he looks healthy. He's scared and worried but looks good to me. Also, I was told the shots are very painful and are given in the stomach for 21 days. The Police and our Doctor say, the chance of Scott getting rabies from that dog are about 1000 to one."

"Have they found the dog, so they can also observe the animal?" questioned Martha.

"No. The building Superintendent who is the owner said it ran away."

"And the Police believe the Superintendent?" said Ellen. "Did they check the basement?"

"Yes. The Police checked all over and even looked in his apartment. You know, this whole thing has made me crazy. I'm so nervous that I've nearly gone out of my mind with worry. It really wasn't Scott's fault. He said they were playing box ball in front of the building and his ball bounced through the fence into the basement area by the coal shoot.

Quietly so he wouldn't disturb the Superintendent whose apartment is right there, Scott climbed down the steps, bent to pickup the ball and a dog came rushing out of the alley, tearing into his right calf muscle. Then Scott began to yell and ran up the steps as fast as he could to get away from the dog. Fortunately, the dog did not chase after Scott; the dog stood its ground and kept barking. Now there is a deep gash where the dog bit Scott. The doctor said it will probably scar."

"What did Larry say about all of this? Did he also agree not to have the shots?" wondered Ellen.

"Yes. Larry came home right after it happened and we both brought Scott to the family doctor. After hearing what the Doctor had to say about the pain involved with the rabies shots, Larry and I made the decision to wait it out. Now as the days drag along, I'm worried if I did the right thing?"

"What did Scott say about not taking the shots?" questioned Martha.

"Well he's real scared and has relied upon us to make the right decision. Since this whole thing has happened, I've kept Scott in bed so I can keep an eye on him. Every 3 hours or so I take his temperature and check his mouth. At the first sign of symptoms, the Doctor said rush Scott to the hospital. You know, the older the kids get, the more I wish I had raised potatoes. Certainly, they are less work and at least I would have some time for myself. Many is the day; I wish I had chosen a career instead of a family."

"You can't mean that you wish you never had a family," said Martha. "Look at how lucky you are. You have a husband who loves you and three healthy sons. Many people would envy your position, you know, including me."

"I know Martha, sometimes you must wish you had a family of your own, but sometimes I wish I had not given-up on what I wanted. In some ways, getting married was an easy way for me not to face what I wanted for myself in life. At least, both you and Ellen have careers as teachers and Ellen has both, a career and a family. Perhaps if I went after what I wanted, I wouldn't feel so bad about myself and we would have more money."

At this point feeling uncomfortable about what Rosetta was saying, Ellen gently inquired, "If you were to do it over again, what kind of career would you have wanted?"

Rosetta paused for a moment, then replied. "Often, I think I gave-up too early on myself, and should have persisted and become a dancer. I shouldn't have listened to the others and kept-up with the training. If I couldn't make it on the stage, I could have at the very least been a dance instructor. Or you know how much I love clothing and fixing myself up, perhaps something in the fashion business. I love glitz and glamour. Struggling like we are and tending after three sons, believe me is far from Broadway and not very glamorous. Particularly 'at friggin' times like this, when I am worried if my eldest son will live out the week."

Then Rosetta began to softly cry and her two sisters, reached over and held her hands.

Manhattan, 1956

Scott and the family survived the rabies scare and it was a time to celebrate. Today the family was going swimming, taking a day trip to Sabego Lake. Rosetta packed a picnic lunch, Larry put gas in the car, and everyone was on the road by 9 am. It was an hour drive to Rockland County and Harriman State Park; across the George Washington Bridge and up the Palisades Interstate Parkway.

Hitting the open road, above the George on the Jersey side, Larry opened-up the car engine and began traveling along at 55 mph. While Larry was busy driving, the windows were down and everyone was comfortable; and the three boys were relatively quiet in the back seat. This gave Rosetta a few moments alone with her thoughts.

Last week, when Ellen and Martha visited, Rosetta said some pretty powerful and revealing things. She wondered, where had these feelings come from? Did she resent having children and not doing something for herself? Before the pressure, anxiety and worry about Scott, certainly, she thought some of these things. However not all of them. Had the fear and worry driven them to the surface? Did she really mean she wished she had raised potatoes instead of children?

Then Rosetta turned and watched her children as they rested in the backseat, she felt proud, full of love and happy to be a mother. Certainly, being a mother taught you a lot about yourself; it was difficult and rewarding work. Each time you thought about what you wanted, one of the little ones approached with a request for help with something. Then it became your need versus theirs and because they were part of you, invariably they won. Was this wrong? To give-up what you wanted for another? Or was this part of our higher purpose?

Some days Rosetta was unsure, particularly like the other day, when resentment reared its ugly head. Usually this happened when she was stressed and raising three sons produced a lot of stress. Rosetta turned toward Larry and Larry felt Rosetta's gaze, and quickly shot her a loving smile. Then Larry refocused on driving and, in that moment, Rosetta again knew that she loved him and her boys.

At times life was certainly complicated. Was it possible to feel two things at the same time? Could you resent having children and also love them? Could you want a career and be angry with your family for the personal sacrifices you had to make? Did this make you a bad person? Or were these only feelings that came and went? How did you figure out which feeling was true or lasting?

Then all of this thinking began to give Rosetta a headache. To relax, she lit-up a cigarette and reminded herself that too much thinking was not a good thing and today was supposed to be a day of fun celebration.

Chapter VI- Susquehanna Road

Rochester, 1984

Nearly 20 years into their marriage, the American Dream came true for Larry and Rosetta; their family moved into their first house. With the move to Rochester, the boys were excited with the extra space and new lives so far from the hustle and bustle of 178th Street. Here there was a backyard, a laundry and dining room, screened in porch, neighbors and the relative quiet of a suburban street.

From the very beginning, Rosetta was unsure if she could adjust. This new life required she learn to drive a car and leave her birth family. Rosetta realized she was too nervous to drive and would have to rely upon others to get around. This bothered and diminished her independent spirit. Some days she felt abandoned 'in the sticks' without a friend.

Over the years, Rosetta learned to depend more and more upon and enjoy her sisters' company. Just calling over the phone was not enough for her; she missed being with them and traveling by car they were seven hours from Manhattan and travel by plane was very expensive.

In the years on Susquehanna Road, the boys finished high school, entered college and military service, married, divorced and began to raise their own families. For Rosetta, this was a time of learning, a time to bend to life's changing winds and move forward.

This movement came with some difficulty and much personal cost.

Rockaway Queens, 1964

It had not all been a life filled with sorrow. There had been many happy times as well. Fondly she remembered their summers in Rockaway by the beach. Everyone enjoyed the sand, hot sun and cool ocean breeze. At first it was a struggle finding the money for the summer bungalow rental, but Rosetta was tired of the family sweating, being miserable in their apartment over the long hot days and nights. To cool all they had were electric fans which just moved the hot air around; because of old, insufficient wiring air conditioning was not an option.

Finally, she put her foot down and told Larry in no uncertain terms, "I don't care if you have to borrow the money or rob a bank I am not spending another hot summer in this cramped apartment." The next day Larry came home with the money, he asked his boss for an advance on his salary.

Later Rosetta started a vacation club at her bank and in this way for the next 3 summers, their lives were cooler and a whole lot more fun. The boys were outside all day long playing by the water, she had friends to talk with and after work the men had each other to play cards and argue baseball. Then came the move to Rochester.

Rochester, 1984

Feeling increasingly tired and light-headed, Rosetta opened her eyes and looked out the dining room window to see if Larry and her sisters had pulled into the parking lot. No sign of them yet. It had started to rain and the drops fell hard and fast.

Rosetta hoped the rainy weather would not delay their flight; it was often cloudy in Rochester with ample amounts of rain and snow. Something about the Lake Effect cloud and wind patterns.

A sunny day in Rochester was as rare as a day without care. Rosetta slowly got used to the long, cold winter snows and wet spring and summer rains. To her the tears from heaven seemed to fall all the way into her soul and inwardly she reluctantly acknowledged their life-giving property. One life died and another was being born. One had been somewhat joyous and another a long hour of despair. Yet both were necessary and according to the religious were part of the plan.

Rochester, 1984

Looking back, Rosetta had some regrets. Clearly, she wished they had never moved to

Rochester; although many things for Larry, Jet and Scott had improved, she herself had lost much. With Barry it was hard to tell how much he had been negatively affected by life in Rochester. Barry had not started having real problems until he moved to San Francisco, and in Rosetta's mind it was unclear how much this was due to life in Rochester. With Barry, she had always suspected there was a frailty and weakness.

Thinking about Jet and Scott, she wished she had been just a little kinder when they visited last year. Yet her failing health had made her grumpy; with all the visitors, it has been too much to fight through the headaches and jumpiness. Over the years, her nerves had been worn to a frazzle.

When Jet indicated that he was driving to Rochester from Colorado, for his 10th High School Reunion, and was bringing his wife and 2 small children to see where he grew-up, that sounded like a wonderful opportunity to visit. Also when Scott offered to meet everyone with his wife and two young children, a family reunion of sorts was planned. Sadly, Barry was left out because he was having drinking and drug problems.

Getting caught up in the enthusiasm of the moment, and because money was an issue for both Jet and Scott's young families, Rosetta offered to have everyone stay in their 4-room apartment. In her mind it would be like old days, everyone under the same roof. The grand kids could sleep on the floor in sleeping bags and the women and men could have a bedroom. This arrangement turned out to be too much for Rosetta; with the 4 youngsters running around in the cramped space, the many meals prepared in their small kitchen and the long wait for the bathroom, she finally 'melted down.' Reluctantly, Larry had to ask Jet and Scott and their families to leave much earlier than planned. Rosetta just couldn't handle all the activity.

The day before Jet and Scott and their families were set to leave it was a beautiful, sunny late winter day; the kind of the day that teases Spring is just around the corner. The temperatures soared into the low 60's and Jet and Scott and their families packed-up a lunch and went to visit the Beach along Lake Ontario. Later that afternoon, when they came back all of the adults raved about the day they had pushing the children on the swings and watching the waves hit along the lake shore. Feeling the sun on their face, had helped renew them from the long, cold winter and stress of being in a cramped apartment. Also, while everyone was playing on the swings, a local television crew arrived to capture people enjoying this extraordinarily warm, sunny moment for a report on the local evening NEWS.

That evening, as everyone sat around eating and chatting, they watched the NEWS and saw the four grand children playing on the swings; laughing and enjoying the sunshine. This memory of joy and happiness, of her 4 grandchildren enjoying life, made Rosetta smile. O if she had only been well enough to go with them that afternoon and had not asked them to leave. She knew there had been hard feelings about cutting the visit short, but much of this sadness was absorbed, that evening, into the smiles of everyone enjoying the local television report.

In her mind, this was a special, wonderful day.

Rochester, 1984

Brring! Brring! Rosetta heard the phone in the living room. Brring! Brring! "Hold your horses — I'll be there just as soon as

I can." Rosetta moved as fast as she could hoping it wasn't bad news. Maybe it was just Larry calling that the plane was delayed because of the rain.

As she picked up the phone, she could hear the voice on the other end imploring, "Mommy, Mommy are you there?"

Realizing it was Barry, Rosetta was disappointed, knowing this wouldn't be good news.

Slowly she replied, "Yes Barry, I am here. How are you?"

"I hate to do this Mommy, but can you send me more money? I need $200 dollars. My rent is due and my disability check doesn't come in for another week. I had to spend extra on my psychiatric medication. Can you help me out?"

Suspecting this wasn't exactly true, she wondered if he needed money for drugs, "What happened to the money I sent 2 weeks ago? You know Dad doesn't want me to keep sending money. We are getting ready to move and need every penny."

"I'm sorry Mommy but I am in a bad way and if you don't help me out I'm not sure what I will do. They are threatening to evict me and I need to give them something. I can't go out on the street again. I am so depressed. If that happens, I might just end it all!"

Hearing this Rosetta moaned out loud, "O Barry, please don't do that!" Then she whispered into the phone. "I will send you some money."

Feeling faint and barely able to stand or hang-up the phone, Rosetta fell onto the living room sofa and began to sweat.

Outside as the thunder clapped and the rain fell harder, Rosetta felt a sharp pain in her forehead and right temple; it hurt like hell and seemed like a firecracker exploded in her brain. Shakily one hand reached out and gripped the sofa, and the other grabbed at her pounding forehead. Breathing with difficulty and sweat rushing out of all pores, Rosetta wondered what was happening. Was this the end?

After an agonizing few moments, which seemed like an hour, the pain began to subside. Feeling the sweat on her body growing colder, Rosetta slipped more deeply into her world of memories and dreams.

Suddenly gone were her fears and worries; gone was her pain and she was free, at peace and no longer afraid. Was this some kind of dream or something more?

And as she wondered about this, magically, through the rain clouds outside her kitchen window there appeared a stairway of white, glowing light and without hesitating she felt herself drifting effortlessly through the apartment walls toward the beckoning stairs; and as she floated and climbed higher she heard an orchestra begin to play. As she listened to the music, she smiled and her body began to sway and move happily along with the notes. As she laughed and glided upward, she found herself filled with love and thrust out onto a stage of multi-colored lights. These colorful lights were ablaze, and the spotlight was upon her. Without thinking Rosetta began to dance joyously to the music and was filled with renewed energy.

And as she danced and moved, her eyes adjusted to the colorful lights; when she looked out into the audience, she saw hundreds of finely dressed men and women who were standing and applauding.

This ovation caused Rosetta to laugh and smile even more, leaping higher, moving faster in rhythm with the music.

Amidst multiple shouts of "Bravo! Bravo!" Rosetta continued to dance on — one with every living thing.

Finally joining her Higher, authentic self in the Light of Heaven.

Book Two:

Raising A Candle

Magnificent Monastery

For the longest time, I wished that I had a church, temple, mosque or synagogue to attend. I could find no special place that called to my heart and helped my soul sing. In years past, there had always been a place: top of a close by hill; stream just below a reservoir dam; tree lined chapel set beside a lake; shaded path through a nearby park; or an old stone church, late at night, when no other person was there. In these holy places, I learned to hear the quiet whispers that flowed through my heart; some from my soul and others from that distant shore. These moments of joyous, quiet solitude and contemplation filled me with peace, reminding of my far away Home.

And just the other day, it occurred to me that I carried my sacred place with me and that the larger world itself now was my monastery. Each morning when I awoke and breathed deeply, I was calling the Holy Name; and when I went to work or ran errands, I was singing hymns of praise. When I helped another person, I was raising us both into the Light, sipping from the Cup of Life.

And in this magnificent monastery of mine: each is free to come and go; sing and dance; create or destroy; all partners in the Cosmic Plan.

I wonder what this world would be like if each person, consciously, realized that this planet is a Grand Cathedral; and in our own private monastery, whatever we are thinking, doing, saying, creating or destroying is a prayer of sorts; generating an energy, combining with all the other energies, forming a symphony of vibrations, felt on an inner level by every creature in the Universe.
—*SB*

Table of Contents

Part I- Spiritual Journey — 132
   1) Goal of Our Journey 132
   2) The Divine Plan 133
   3) Spiritual Journey 134
   4) Breaking Free 135
   5) Child of the Universe 136
   6) The Wheel of Life 137
   7) Breaking Camp 138
   8) Beginning and Ending 140
   9) The Rainbow Bridge 142
   10) Garden of Life 145
   11) Let Your Soul Soar 147
   12) Why do I Forget? 149
   13) Higher Than Angels 150
   14) How Many Times? 150
   15) Finding Your Own Path 152

Part II- Light & Darkness — 153
   16) Love Song 153
   17) Crazy Poet 154
   18) Part of The Eternal Oneness 154
   19) What the Mystic Knows 155
   20) Why Must It Be So? 157
   21) For You Today 158

22) Spiritual Experience 159
23) Place Of Chains 160
24) Precious Treasure 161
25) Magnificent Meadow 162
26) Celestial Sea 162
27) Raising A Candle 163
28) Happiness 165
29) Opposites 166
30) Hope 166
31) Gradual Enlightenment 170
32) Speaking Plainly 171
33) Only Real Future 172
34) Pure Creative Energy 172

Part III- The Struggle   174
35) Inner War 174
36) Caves of My Mind 175
37) Dark Hour 176
38) What If 177
39) Journey with Hope 179
40) Space Aliens 179
41) Learning Structure 180
42) A Higher Call 181
43) Idols 182
44) New Form 183
45) Journey To the Sun 183
46) Twilight Travel Song 185

47) In This Cell 187
48) A Righteous Heart 187

Part IV- Some Favorites   189
49) Loneliness 189
50) He Shall Walk 190
51) Light of Humanity 191
52) The Songbird 192
53) The Child 193
54) I Wonder Why 194
55) My God Sings 195
56) Repeating Thought Patterns 196
57) The Message 197
58) Desert Tears 198
59) The Eternal Reality 199
60) Bird Cage 200

Part I- Spiritual Journey

1) Goal of Our Journey

>   The Universe is an awfully big
>   And divergent place;
>   Where there is room
>   For all kinds of beings, beliefs
>   And endless realities.
>
>   Yet within this multiplicity
>   There is Oneness and Connection.
>   That is the Goal of our journey.

2) The Divine Plan

In each moment
The Divine Plan is revealed.
With the ticking of each second,
By the clock of time,
We have the opportunity
To reach higher;
Stay where we are
Or follow our lower urges.

Yes. Within each moment
We may choose to ascend;
Help another
And reach upward:
Fulfilling our Cosmic Potential.

3) Spiritual Journey

Consider a drop of water, in its journey to the sea, as it undergoes change.

One day the drop is mist. The next it has become part of a passing cloud. On the third day, the drop falls onto the ground as a raindrop; eventually the drop seeps down into the earth and joins other drops as part of a mountain stream. Eventually this stream winds its way into a river and the river empties, along with the drop, into a mighty ocean.

Now this drop of water as it lies in the ground may be frozen for a time and in the spring thaw join as part of a lovely flower. In time the moisture in the flower evaporates back into the air and the drop, again, becomes part of a passing cloud. However, in this next cycle, it falls on the earth as part of a winter snow. Eventually the drop melts and seeps into the ground. Gradually it resumes the journey of finding its way to the mountain stream, river and ocean.

Throughout the journey, the drop changes many times, assumes different roles and learns about itself in a variety of ways. When it joins the ocean, the drop will be that much more complete and conscious of its potential. It is always a drop of water.

In part this is the nature of the soul's journey through the many worlds. One of the differences between our journey as humans is that we are able to show many more physical changes and manifestations of ourselves. The outcome our souls seek is to be complete and reach their highest potential through the many changes.

4) Breaking Free

>Each of us
>Builds walls around us
>To hide away our fears.
>Our daily patterns of work and play
>Can be jailers which bind
>Our true, lasting nature.
>
>Of what are we afraid?
>
>O fragile one,
>We are the caterpillar
>Who is too timid
>To break out of the cocoon.

5) Child of the Universe

Each of us
Is an eternal Child of the Universe.
Traveling from world to world
Living on
As Beings of conscious energy;
Creating one adventure after another.

In our present form
We are bound by physical laws.
When sickness and death enter
We forget for a time
Our individual greatness and invincibility.
Caught-up in the moment
Of pain and suffering.
Wondering why
It has to be this way?

O Child of Light
Remember this is but one port of call.
One stop of endless possibility
Along the glorious voyage Home.

Here we explore
The many aspects of Creation;
Learning, partners in the Divine Plan.

6) The Wheel of Life

What once was
Will no longer be
And cannot be again.

What is developing
Is another form.
Another variation.
A new spoke
On the Wheel of Life.

Turning, turning, always, turning.
Giving and taking
Moving upward and creating.
Join in the Wheel's motion
Or be still,
What does it matter?
The Wheel keeps turning.

You wonder
What lies behind this turning?
What is its Source?
That my friend is the mystery.

Few seek to solve this mystery
Or break free of the timeless motion.
These are the travelers of the Heart
And the road traveled
Passes through
The place of non-being.

7) Breaking Camp

It is almost time to leave;
The heat from yesterday's fire
Drops to a low, quiet burn.
The last few hours

I work to leave this site
Better than when I found it.
As I pick through scattered debris,
I wonder, what is next?

In this new place, will old friends
Help and greet me?
Or will I be on my own?
O the sadness of breaking camp weighs heavily,
And has not been replaced,
By anticipation for the new.

Each stop
Another step
Along the road Home.
Another place to set-up camp,
Celebrate, dance and enjoy
Breathing deep the clean, fresh mountain air.

Over the years, I've heard many tales
About the new place,
Wondering: what actually will be there?
Walking through this mountain forest,
Singing my song of change,
I am free to reach upward
And embrace the Oneness
That is all about me.

8) Beginning and Ending

Breaking apart, the acorn
Goes deep into the earth;
And as the seasons pass
Grows into a mighty oak.
Spreading its limbs for many years,
Giving shade and nourishment to the countryside;
One day, only to decay

And return back to the earth.

O spiritual traveler, when you close your eyes
For the last time, where will you go?

The dual sparks of energy
That joined and exploded
Inside your mother's womb,
Carry you through your days.
Then one day, this energy too
Must journey on to the next place.

Where will this life energy take you?

Remember, it was Love
That brought you here,
And Love will carry you
From world to world;
Finally to return Home
And celebrate anew
In your Mother's Arms.

9) The Rainbow Bridge

    Every child grows-up
    Hoping to claim the treasure
    At the end of the rainbow bridge.

    On those rare days, after the storm,
    Magically the rainbow appears — gladdening each heart.
    The sky is renewed with a variety of colors
    And each child dreams
    Of traveling their favorite color
    In search of the pot of gold.

    Within each heart
    The hope is eternal
    We can transcend our fears
    And arrive at our heart's desire.

Yes, like the rainbow
Within each soul
There is a glorious bridge
To the eternal riches.
For each temperament there is a path;
And the journey, on an inner level,
Consists of embracing the different colors.

The rainbow has its origin in the storm;
For without the wind and rain
The colors would not reflect.
Each color represents the seasons of a soul;
And to every heart there is a season of love.
The traveler who seeks the Light
Must journey all the seasons of their heart.

Some say

This life is ravaged by storms;
Remember they speak the truth
As they see it.
This life is shaded by dark colors:
But the Light is waiting to reflect
Upon each heart.
If you ask the Beloved
She will show you the treasure
That is waiting in your soul.

And when the Light begins to shine
Upon your heart;
Your journey through this world
Will be a celebration of colors.
You will join the rainbow
And travel to the horizon
And be greeted by the Lord.

Like the rainbow-
Prayer is a bridge

To the hidden riches.

In the quiet of the evening

And the early hours of the morning-

Sing God's praise.

Journey on-

Following the colors in your heart.

And as God Wills

One day

You will become the hidden treasure;

Having embraced all the colors of your heart-

And you will have become the rainbow bridge.

10) Garden of Life

The superior gardener works from an inner feeling;

Intuitively knowing what needs to be done.

Songs Against the Darkness

Having studied, tended and planted for years;
The garden and gardener are One.

The plants, insects, birds and animals,
All part of this work
And come together
With the earth, rain and sun
To form a living system.
Ever changing and developing;
This small universe
Is an extension
Of the gardener's own inner song.

Like gardens, travelers are linked
Through an interplay of events and factors.
Remember — we are all rare flowers
That have the potential
To open to the sun,
And grace the morning breeze

With a unique, perfumed fragrance.

This is particularly true,
As we connect with our higher nature.

11) Let Your Soul Soar

Chained to a world of illusion
Created by others and my desires;
How hollow are these dreams?

My soul cries out:
Fly away. Soar above these fences.
Go Higher. You are a Child of Light.

Rush toward the stars.
Go beyond the Sun.
There is your Home;
In the Nameless, timeless

Land that you have forgotten.

You are a Prince
And have come here
For a brief moment.
Let you soul soar, again,
Higher than the eagles,
Higher than the angels.

You are the son of a King
And seek to embrace
All that is yours.
A timeless Spiritual Traveler
Who creates Reality
Upon Reality
All in the Name
Of that which is greatest.

12) Why do I Forget?

I lift my cup
And sip Your Wine.
You are there to comfort me;
And fill me with peace.
Every place I turn
There is bitterness.
At first there may have been joy,
But it always turns bitter in the end.

Why do I forget?
Nothing is lasting except God.

Thank you for being patient
And filling my cup, again.

13) Higher Than Angels

In this world, because of the demands and pleasures
Of the physical body, many travelers loose sight
Of the soul's long journey back to the Source.

Yet, if we are somehow able
To transcend this physical pull, even for an instant,
We are able to soar higher than the angels.

14) How Many Times?

I wonder how many times
I have walked upon this planet.

Certainly this is not my first trip;

I am an old-time traveler who has returned, building upon past vacations.

Sometimes I wonder why I put myself through this journey again and again.

The flesh decays; sunshine turns to darkness and those you love pass away.

Why return to this place of sorrow and tragedy?

Yet the heart whispers — because without bitterness there can be no sweetness.

Without loneliness there can be no love.

Without death there can be no life.

All to be shared, over and over again;

All to know the Creator, myself and others more fully.

Personally joining in the act of Creation-moment by moment.

15) Finding Your Own Path

Each person must find their own wisdom and way to Truth.

In the spiritual journey, while the guidance, writing and exercises of others help another find their way; and can even be an essential factor in overall success, still, these are not a substitute for personal spiritual experience.

Ultimately it is the Unseen Forces and Grace of the Path, which enable a traveler to experience and find their own path to the Light.

Part II- Light & Darkness

16) Love Song

I want to leave you with a song that will set your soul afire and lead you back to the land from which you came. This song has been playing since time was an idea carried on the universal wind. This song resides in the deep stillness of your soul and takes on a melody when you breathe out the notes.

Come my children — sing out with me so we might bring forth a resounding chorus to make the heavens weep and flowers bloom in the sweet sun shower of eternal light.

Then all children of the universe will be at peace, singing in the empyrean Light of humanity's greatest achievement . . . their own love song.

17) Crazy Poet

My gift to you are these words which, from time to time, appear on these pages.

Often they originate on a distant shore, where Celestial Light is a morning sun, and a gentle breeze ushers their energy softly through me. The Author is that Radiance which has created an Ocean of Wisdom that has always been.

Today if these words have no meaning for you, then, forget or perhaps store them in a drawer for later. It is my hope, that at some point, they please and enrich you; lifting you-up higher on your journey Home.

These words are eternal, transcribed with ink that never dries. As the Universe wills, may you benefit from their notes. If you listen with an inner ear: you will sing and fill with joy.

Me, I am but a scribe, a crazy poet, dancing madly through this long starry night.

18) Part of The Eternal Oneness

In order to create and maintain our body, each person is a killer and destroyer. Daily consuming thousands of living organisms: fish, plant, vegetables, animals, grains and in our water countless microorganisms.

So in every act of creation, we are destroying, altering and changing; evolving one form into another. Here in this moment both actions: creation and destruction the same; part of the Eternal Oneness.

And when we journey on to the next place our physical and spiritual form returns to the timeless ether from which we originate; particles of Cosmic Fabric interweaving, evolving and altering yet again: part of the Eternal Oneness.

19) What the Mystic Knows

> When looking at the world
> Darkness and Light:
> That is the way
> It has always been;
> With a thousand shades
> Of color in between.

Songs Against the Darkness

In this moment
Where do you stand?
Are you a radiance
Of the Light
Or a shade of Darkness?

O spiritual traveler,
Hark, you are both
Of these things
And many more.
Ascend to your greatness.
Access the Divine
Creator within you.

Call the Name
And become One
With the timeless
Loving Energy
That flows through you
And all things.

Then, you will have transcended
Darkness and Light,
Time and Space;
Becoming a golden spoke
On the Wheel of life.

20) Why Must It Be So?

My heart cries out: why must it be so?
The flower petal decays and the seed gently falls onto the earth.
Slowly, the seed burrows into the dirt reaching for nutrients and protection;
Over time, combining with different elements:
Straining to bring forth another flower.

In the spring sunshine, the flower's fragrance opens to the wind

And the meadow again shares in a timeless dance.

O man, you and this flower are forever joined;

Brothers and sisters of the Eternal Cycle

Of Hope, Oneness and Renewal.

O spiritual traveler, why be sad?

Tomorrow you will again lift up your arms

And celebrate in the glorious sunshine:

Calling all manner of creatures

To join your timeless celebration of rebirth.

21) For You Today

For you today, what I wish
Is that you sit quietly, for a moment,
And go deep within yourself.

There amidst the chatter and worry
Is a deep quiet, loving place
That is your center.
Find this place. It is there. Don't give-up.

It is the treasure you have been seeking,
And is waiting for you to pick-it-up
And use its miraculous powers;
To transform yourself
And make this world
A planet of sunshine, love,
Abundance and caring for each other.

Remember, one by one
We reach higher,
And help others
Drink deeply
And embrace our Collective Potential.

22) Spiritual Experience

I cannot give you
Spiritual experience;

This is something
This arises from within you
And is bestowed by the Unseen Forces.

Yet, I can remind you
That you must work
And strive
To seek the highest
In every action.

Then, as the Universe Wills
The flood gates shall open
And spiritual caresses
Shall flow outward
Like honey from the hive.

23) Place Of Chains

I am weary of things that bind. Some call them: treasures, responsibilities of life, enjoyments, everyday thoughts and activities of eating and living.

    O I long to be free again: flying on the wind. Once I was a hawk and another time a dragon. This time, I am a mouse scurrying from room to room: searching for crumbs and excitement.

Let me shatter this trance and immerse myself in the River. The River will guide me to my next adventure; leaving this place of self-imposed chains, far behind.

24) Precious Treasure

The moment of a person's death is fixed.

What is not constant

Is how we spend our lives.

Remember, use these hours well.

They are as precious as any treasure

You will ever find.

25) Magnificent Meadow

Remember, this moment is all we have; we are not promised another. While another may follow, it is always a gift from the Universe. In this moment do something wonderful: laugh, sing, shout out loud, jump for joy, extend a hand to help another, offer a prayer of thankfulness. And if unable to celebrate because of illness, pain or worry: call out to the One who has Given this opportunity — to open Her arms and bestow a healing caress upon your heart.

Never forget, each is a Child of the Universe, on a glorious voyage of self discovery, wonder and thanks. May our moments be flowers opening to the sun and rain, always proclaiming our life in this magnificent meadow.

26) Celestial Sea

    O spiritual traveler,

    Of what are you created?

    Flesh and bone

    Is only part of the answer.

Remember, you are also of Spirit
And will wake-up one day to find
You have joined the morning sun;
Lighting up a celestial sea.

27) Raising A Candle

From time to time
I have to remember
Why I came here.
So often the passing days
Cause me to forget.
You see I hold in my hand
A candle, with a brilliant flame,
To fight the growing darkness.

Yet when aglow
I raise my candle high

So others might see,
And the Light blinds them.
They run away, holding their eyes,
Shaking their head, confused.

So what am I to do?

Still I raise my candle
Waiting for the weary traveler
Who needs a Light
To find their Way.
Then, as indicated,
I touch my candle to theirs
And together we travel
Illuminating the dark night.

28) Happiness

Traveler: And the traveler sat before the Master and questioned, "Happiness is a transitory thing. It is as illusive as a spring day in winter. One moment I am laughing and the next sad. Master tell me what I must do to balance myself and find lasting happiness?"

Master: And the Master sat, with eyes closed, for what seemed like an hour to the young student. Finally the Master opened his eyes and softly spoke, "True and lasting happiness is found by immersing yourself in the river of your soul and, when the water has changed you, helping others. One of the great ones has said, 'A happy man thinks happy thoughts.' Yet how do you get to a place where you think only happy thoughts? That is the mystery. It was not until I immersed myself in my own river and was changed, did I fully understand how this was possible."

In the ensuing silence, the traveler wondered how long he had to swim in the water of his own soul before he experienced a personal answer.

29) Opposites

The sparrows play and flutter about in the dirt.

Flapping their wings

They cleanse themselves with the soil.

If we did this

We would become dirty.

Requiring water to accomplish

This very same task,

We wonder how cleansing is possible?

Yet the same objective

May be reached by different means;

Sometimes they appear as opposites.

30) Hope

There is a story about a youth

Who lived in a land of darkness.

Dr. Stewart Bitkoff

And in this land
No one had ever seen Light.
This youth was different than his friends;
In the quiet of the endless darkness
He would hear whispers
That seemed to originate from within his heart.
These whispers urged him to climb the mountains
That surrounded his home, and wait.

For many years, this fellow gave little thought
To the inner voice and its promise.
He continued his everyday affairs
And at the end of the week, as was the custom,
Would indulge every sensory whim.

Finally after years of indulgence
In the midst of a drunken stupor

He was awakened by the inner voice.

> *You choose darkness to Light.*
> *You are foolish.*
> *With the sunrise*
> *Is the promise of the Lord.*

And with these words the drunkenness left.

Impulsively this fellow began to run toward the mountains.

With the urgency of a lover

In flight to his beloved,

He scaled the mountains

And began to wait.

After many hours, the silence was broken

And the inner voice commanded.

> *Turn toward the east.*
> *The Light shall be revealed*
> *And you will know the promise*

Of your Lord.

And amidst the darkness of his world
The Light was revealed.
From that moment
He became foremost in faith.

As the sunrise is heralded
By faint rays of Light,
So, hope is eternal
Tomorrow will be brighter.

Although this world is filled with darkness;
Hope waters the heart of each believer.
For He that created the darkness
Also created the Light,
And darkness and light follow each other.

31) Gradual Enlightenment

Learn to see those things
Which you must do
And those things
Which God must do?
The spiritual traveler who recognizes the difference
Is on their way to enlightenment.

Most travelers expect enlightenment
To arrive in a flash of over whelming awareness.
They imagine it is like turning on
A lamp in their home.
This is our expectation and desire for haste;
This stems from our greed.

For most, the enlightenment process is much slower
And knowledge comes in stages.

And once the Light is on
It cannot be turned off
As easily as hitting a switch.

32) Speaking Plainly

Each traveler is immortal and comes into the earth phase to know, experience and create self in infinite ways. Taking on a physical body, in a sense the soul forgets for a time, that it is an eternal spark of Light.

At it's center, this primal Oneness continues, even though the soul, forgetting, assumes other identities.

Because you are a child of Light: you are in fact part of Light and will always be this.

33) Only Real Future

The only real future for the human race
Is to act as mature human beings
Who love and care for each other.

As a planet, we must be in the business of making better people
And support all enterprises that truly have this as their goal.

Collectively this must be our Great Work;
A planet of loving, caring and helpful people
Who rise above their own lower nature
And reach toward the heavens, clasping their neighbor's hand.

34) Pure Creative Energy

There is a life giving and sustaining element in the Universe that is pure creative energy. It is in everything, has consciousness and is the basis for what we know as Reality. It has potential and endless ways of expressing itself; part of this energy is in you and me: it is the inner fabric of each cell and our life source.

The mystic calls this energy the Light; others have named it the Source, the heart, or in ages past: God. This energy is the basis of religion and is our primal center; recreating our body, our awareness and reality, daily. This is the part that will lead us on to the next place.

The mystics have embraced this primal energy since the beginning of time; have learned to use it in their daily lives and pass this knowing on to others who are capable of using it.

Today our scientists have begun to suspect that this Ultimate Creative Element is a Reality; in some circles it is even becoming common knowledge, and more and more the average person is beginning to embrace this concept of Universal Oneness.

Yet where do we go from here?
You and I must decide.

Part III- The Struggle

35) Inner War

> The hardest battles
> Are not fought in fields
> Or on seas, but within ourselves.
>
> We are the enemy
> Who ravages
> Every defenseless position

Dr. Stewart Bitkoff

36) Caves of My Mind

How long is this sentence?
Jailed in a world
Of my own creation.

Afraid to break free;
Daily I am tormented
By thoughts and desires.
These rub against me
Like thorns from a tree.

You say: leave them behind.
Move on. You are what
Stands in your way!

O that it were that easy.
Old thoughts, like chains pulling at me.
Wearisome, repetitious living,
In the dark caves of my mind.

O Lord, help me break free

And journey back into the Light;

Leaving myself behind, again.

37) Dark Hour

O spiritual traveler, I fear these are dark times

In which the lower self has risen

To take the place of the higher.

Where is the Light for this dark hour?

Look closer. It is there.

Turn inward and embrace

Your own personal beacon for the long night.

It is the song in your heart — remembering —

You are a ray of Light from a Grand Sun.

Rejoice, rise higher.
Your inner Light shall guide you
Through this world and into the next.

38) What If

What if all the money, energy, thought and time
Used for war and countries fighting each other
Was used to feed the hungry, care for the sick
And help those in need?

Yes, what if all across the world
Soldiers, sailors and fliers
Turned their attention and energy
Toward healing and building
Instead of defending and fighting?

And what if, in every land,

The manufacturers of guns and weapons

Used their resources to build homes for the homeless

And hospitals for the sick and dying?

Can you imagine such a world?

That's the world we should be reaching to manifest.

Ask any soldier which is a better choice — life or death;

Yet many are not ready to abandon their old ways.

This way of killing and fear serves individual purpose.

How long will it take for humanity to learn the lesson?

The choice to build or destroy

Is ours, collectively,

Every moment of every day.

39) Journey with Hope

Sometimes when considering problems, because of our finite nature, it appears as if there are no further solutions and our prayers will not be answered.

Yet because there is another level — the world of spirit with its boundless love and mercy — there is always tomorrow, endless possibility and another sunrise.

Travel on my brothers and sisters: in truth we do not fully know what tomorrow brings.

The Light beckons, "Weary traveler remember to journey with hope, and Our Promise of love, joy and mercy."

40) Space Aliens

    Just like in science fiction,
    Sometimes I think
    The only time
    The human race
    Will work together is if the earth
    Were attacked by space aliens;

And we all have to join hands
To fight off the oppressors.

Yes, to survive in a calamity,
We have no other choice:
But to cooperate with each other.

41) Learning Structure

In many things, discipline and hard work are essential.

In higher studies, these attributes provide a structure

Through which other things may develop and flourish.

And always, it is a matter of Grace and destiny.

42) A Higher Call

Make no mistake about it life is hard;
Filled with pain, illness, struggle
And eventual death.

Yet a remedy to this circumstance
Is love and passion:
Passion for what you wish to be or do;
Love for another person;
Or love of a Higher Calling.

When the night is dark
And you are lost in a haze,
Suddenly the sun rises
And shows you the way back Home, again.

For most, this life is a journey of the flesh;
Both glorious and frightening.
Remember, this duality exists

So that you might rise Higher.
You are a Child of both worlds
And are set free through love;
Embrace your destiny.
You cannot escape it.

43) Idols

One day, sit down
And list all the things
You are concerned and worry about.
Make a list
And leave nothing out.

These things
Which comprise your worry list
Are your 'idols' or 'false gods.'
They are the thoughts
Which fill your mind-
Instead of the Eternal.

44) New Form

When the potter is forming a bowl
And it has a defect,
Which cannot be repaired,
What does she do?
Keeping the clay,
The potter starts anew.

O spiritual traveler,
The hour of change is upon us.
That which will be kept
Is essential to the New Form.

45) Journey To the Sun

How foolish I have been.
Like a moth that tried to fly
To close to the candle's flame, got singed

And returned, wanting to share with others
This life changing event:
Being united, embracing his Love.
I too have been altered
By the Light of another flame.

Now, wandering on this street corner,
Fumbling to tell my story to anyone who will listen.
Worse than laughter, I am ignored
And left alone, to silently remember;
My brief journey to the sun.

Perhaps I will stand quietly
Reliving that glorious hour
When, for an instant, I touched Infinity.
Yet the pain and distance
Of not going further
Still tears away at my heart,

Not letting me rest.

Alone, left to limp along,
Living in yesterday's rapture and pain;
Continually calling out to my Beloved:
When will you touch my heart, again?

46) Twilight Travel Song

As I travel in twilight
My mind is filled
With memories of days long past;
Friends, co-workers, forgotten;
People loved
And joyful holidays.

Now I am visited
By different friends.
These fill me with pain

And disease:
Taking youth and vigor.

You know, the wise claim
Pain is part of us.
Reminding
Where we came from
And where we will be
Upon the morrow.
I try not to dwell on these things.
Leaving them for more peaceful
Songs of the heart;
Slowly leading me on
To another home.

Today like a fragile butterfly
I feel the cold wind shatter my wings,
And shiver
In the fading twilight.

47) In This Cell

In this cell, I sit day after day.
It is not the cell of cloistered monk
Or political prisoner. Far from that.
It is the world of repetitious living.

Sadly, I am the jailer
Who has forgotten the key.
Frightened, I will get familiar with the darkness
And no longer seek the Light.

48) A Righteous Heart

Spiritual learning is in addition to all your many skills/talents.

It is intended as the center of a life from which all other aspects nourish and mature.

You were created to participate in the world and help make it better. That is the potential; that is the goal.

Spiritual learning does not replace other skills and abilities. It enhances their effectiveness and enables a fuller life.

Consider that there is difference between spiritual learning and what some come to know as religion. The inner core of all religion is spiritual learning; in some situations, this learning occurs without religion.

A righteous heart is always a flower for the world to enjoy.

Part IV- Some Favorites

49) Loneliness

O Lord, now I see
Why You created humanity.
What a lonely place
This earth can be.

When the house is empty
And those you love have gone,
It is so quiet.
Loneliness can weigh heavily on a heart.

O Lord, our laughter and smiles
Are joys to You.
Humanity provides the wings
Upon which Your heart can soar.

50) He Shall Walk

And he shall walk among us again.
His presence shall sing of breezes
From mountain streams;
Touching hearts with a loving caress.

All men and women shall bow before his majesty
And ask forgiveness for their fears.
He shall awaken a realization, never known,
Of the Creator's Mercy.
Men and women shall weep
In the arms of their fellows.

Nations that were parted
Shall be joined,
And all people shall again be One
With the Father.

51) Light of Humanity

The diversity of humanity amazes me.
There are more people
Than stars in the night sky.
More blood flows
Through the hearts of man and woman
Than water splashes
Against the river shore.

Imagine if each heart
Were aglow with love.
The Light would shine
Across the galaxy.

God would turn
To the angels and proclaim:
The Light of humanity
Is the morning sun.
Prepare my chariot,
My children await me!

52) The Songbird

Traveler: "Master, please help me, I have pondered the riddle and my mind aches from trying to work out the answer."
Master: "Little one, the mind was not created to work out this problem; the answer comes from the heart. The mind's job is to ask. Since you have worked, struggled and now requested assistance, I will provide the answer."

> "It matters not to the songbird
> if other birds are there to hear its song.
> The song and sweet melody
> arise from the heart and the notes must
> be sung.

The mountains, lakes, flowers and streams
sway to the bird's song;
they listen with an inner ear.

It is the same
with a traveler's life.
Each has a song to sing
and it matters not
if others are there
and hear the tune.

For it is the song of creation;
This song must be sung
and in the singing is the joy."

53) The Child

And so they came

To see the child.

The miracle had occurred

And they were drawn

To share in the beginning.

Bearing gifts they came,

Singing praise to their King.

This child was born
To dance among humanity
And turn heads upward in remembrance.

And with Her breath
This life began
And in each heart
A candle is waiting.

This child was born
To carry the flame.

54) I Wonder Why

Sometimes I wonder why
There are so many people,
And why

There are thousands of birds,
And why
The earth is filled with insects,
And why
The ocean has all those fish,
And why
The land nourishes plants,
And why
There are so many things
I can't name them all.

O Lord, is this endless variety
To convince us You exist?

55) My God Sings

My God sings on the breeze.

I am the darkness

And I am the light.
I am the sun
And I am the rain.
I am your love
And I am your pain.

I am the stars
And I am the seas.
I am you
And you are me.

My God invites me
To join the celebration
And dance to the notes of creation.

56) Repeating Thought Patterns

Each spiritual traveler's consciousness is a series of repeating patterns which are like the rooms of a fine house. Each room is decorated with paint, curtains, furniture and other chosen pieces. While these trappings reflect the owner's individuality, the room is bedroom, dining room or kitchen. It has a function which combines with the others to make up the house.

Often we become jailers, content to live our life in these rooms only. We never consider there may be another world beyond these walls. That is why each house has a door. The wise learn to use it.

57) The Message

The message has always been the same. We are the ones who have forgotten. The religion is one and humanity has a common Source. Over time, because people are different culturally, messengers and religious forms vary. This confuses people.

The Light is the binding force of the universe and is the mother and father of us all. It is the great river from which we all came. On the surface, the river's water shifts due to changing currents and wind. Yet beneath the surface the water remains calm and tranquil.

In this age, people are frightened and searching for something to help ease their fear and unite them. It is there, but we have forgotten to go deep and embrace our common spiritual heritage.

Within each, the Light is waiting to bring us Home and illumine the darkness.

58) Desert Tears

And he went into the desert to find the answers.

He looked into the sky and began to ask,

And the days passed.

When no answers came

He looked out across the land and asked again,

And the days passed.

When he realized the desert could not answer,

Tears from the heart began to fill his eyes.

And the tears fell like spring rain

Forming a small pool at his feet.

And he looked into the water

And watched the sands drink of his suffering.

Then the answers came.

59) The Eternal Reality

And the day will come
When all the things
We cherished
Will have passed.

We shall stand naked
Before the King
And He will ask:
What remains?

And from the depth
Of our heart
Will arise a loving whisper:
O Lord, You are the Eternal Reality.

60) Bird Cage

> Like a captive bird
> The soul sings,
> Remembering its home.
>
> It is precisely
> For this song,
> The bird is caged.

Appendix:

How to be Spiritual Amidst this Chaos?

How to be Spiritual Amidst this Chaos?
By Dr. Stewart Bitkoff

> *Circumstances have overtaken man. His old languages are not sufficient to describe what is happening, and what is about to happen. To think in terms of a millennium or such tame concepts as 'the eleventh hour' is ridiculous. Better that he should realize that he is in an era which might be more accurately described as the 'eighth day of the week.'*
>
> —*Idries Shah*

For the spiritual traveler, we are living in a complex and unique age. There is tremendous upheaval yet great opportunity to come together and solve problems. Turn on the television set or the internet and listen to the reports of "bad news" coming in from all across the globe: a world wide pandemic rages, in many countries there are protests against the police and their racial policies, religious wars continue, effects of global warming are destroying our environment, many people are starving, new strains of disease are emerging, drug wars continue and over weight children fill our technological consciousness.

While advances in technology have caused problems they are also a tool for people to work together to solve them. Personal technology, like cell phones and access to social media, has made more visible many of our previously 'hidden' social and economic villains. This combination of factors has been called the 'eighth day of the week' and the beginning of a new era; clearly, until many of these problems are resolved, if that is possible, the amount of unsettledness, fear, anxiety and personal worry for many will continue to grow.

For increasing numbers of people, the personal balancing factor to this stress and chaos, is spiritual development. It must be added to the mix and used with our other capacities to find solutions. Higher knowledge will not replace common sense, experience, hard work or economic imperative. That is not its function. It is an added capacity which integrates and works alongside others.

The present discussion will examine some basic thoughts about being spiritual; and how spiritual capacity can help the traveler deal with this period of chaos and change.

What Does It Mean To Be Spiritual?

What does the term spiritual mean? Spiritual is not an easy word to define, because there is an experiential aspect to it, with many levels and dimensions. Sort of like love, which is a sublime experience and occurs in many forms; poets and song writers proclaim its virtues and sorrows, yet, no matter how fine the words, they are only an approximation.

Typical definitions include phrases such as: *spiritual means of the spirit.* This type of definition: defines itself using the same word, yet, surprisingly is reasonably accurate. *Spiritual does mean of the spirit.*

For the spiritual traveler, the soul is comprised of a spiritual energy fabric; this spiritual energy is the source of life and powers our body, 5 senses, emotions and consciousness. To the soul, there is a higher and lower aspect which corresponds to different parts of our functioning (physical, mental, emotional, and spiritual); to further complicate matters, in some discussions the terms soul and spirit are used interchangeably.

- The goal of spiritual paths, or *being spiritual,* is to add a measure of conscious spiritual awareness to the traveler's individual life and day; this knowledge or awareness serves as an enriching, enabling element, so the traveler can complete daily and higher functions.

- For the most part, everyday activity, work and worry block the inner (spiritual) awareness from coming forward.

- All life operates through consciousness, which for humans is awareness and energy on multiple physical, mental, emotional and spiritual levels. Through our soul, which is comprised of this spiritual energy fabric, we create our multiple levels of reality, every moment of the day.

- Each one of us is a creator of reality. We are souls that have taken on a physical form to create our lives and participate in the higher design. In order to do this, we must follow a spiritual path and lead a balanced life.

- A full life is a life where we express all the parts of self and participate in something higher.

- Increased spiritual capacity helps the traveler *know* what is going on around them; this knowledge helps them on a daily basis.

Characteristics of a Spiritual Person

Another way to help define spiritual is to examine personality traits of spiritual people. These characteristics help us get a better understanding of what it means to be spiritual in daily life, however, there are problems here as well; while these traits are accurate, also, they can be said to exist in non-spiritual people:

- Spiritual people have a sense of humor and are not 'stuffy old farts'- and they enjoy laughing;
- Spiritual people are involved in their community and may work and raise a family;
- Spiritual people seek to help others as much as themselves;
- They are free with their time and energy — volunteer their efforts;
- A spiritual person demonstrates continual striving to get better;
- A spiritual person lives by their conscience;

- They try to live a life that is free of *expectation* and *comparison* to others;

- They try to look at different issues from a broad framework and respect the ideas of others;

- They are not on a power trip or trying to control the ideas and lives of others;

- Spiritual values are long held and they are genuinely humble.

While the spiritual traveler acknowledges problems in definition and realizes they are seeking an elusive essence, there is another part of the consciousness that offers: 'do not worry: you will know it, when you find it.' Like love, spiritual defines itself and by adding this capacity to your life, your life will be fuller, more complete and you will be better able to face life's ups and downs.

Routine Change or the End?

Through increased information that is available via television and the internet, the average person viewing the unrest in our world cannot help but wonder: what is going on? Conversely scientists and philosophers tell us chaos and order are simply opposite ends of a continuum. Both are natural to life and necessary to the physical order. And so the spiritual traveler wonders: is this era simply a routine period of unrest — soon to be followed by a period of relative calm?

Consider the following themes and ideas and how each contributes to our fear and growing anxiety level. Each of which can be found either in your religious/spiritual belief system or on your local television programs, nightly and weekly.

- Many religious or spiritual paths discuss a destruction/ending of sorts — of which many scenarios seem to coincide with this time period. Is this the end of the world? Also current scientifically based television shows describe 'end of world' natural disasters, questioning: will the world shift on its axis? Will a large meteor hit the earth? Through global warming, will we send the earth into another ice-age? When will the next super volcano erupt? Often these shows include prophetic references: are these events the earth changes that Cayce and other prophets have described?

- Some belief systems hold that previously there have been 4 destructions of the earth. The Mayan Calendar ended in year 2012; according to Sufi Tradition, the Stream of Life has dried-up and will be replaced with the new Stream of Life. Destruction and rebirth- natural cycles that have occurred many times?

- Recently, across the world, there has been a failure of government and large corporations to solve economic problems and react in a timely manner to natural disasters; also, for the average person, these institutions appear to have been at the center of many of the ills that affect us. As a result, gradually, many are turning away from reliance upon authoritarian based models to individual based structures. Slowly we are collectively realizing that neither governments nor corporations nor religion alone can save us; we must all work to make the world better and begin this effort with ourselves.

- More people are solving problems locally and gradually realizing that the world is made better one person at a time; this is the person-centered approach. Additionally there is growing interest in spiritual paths that emphasize personal development. Better individuals make a better world.

- Personal, corporate, and governmental greed, along with religious fanaticism increasingly are threats to our way of life.

- Honoring the Earth Mother or destruction of the environment; how will it end? Will we pull together or destroy the planet?

- Information explosion: boon or curse? How 'others' manipulate us by giving and withholding information to support their own agendas.

Understanding Emotion: Love and Fear

By nature, we are emotional and our reactions to life, through multiple feelings contribute to a richer, full experience. When something happens in daily life that is painful we all have a reaction to it. We are multi-level beings and our emotions bring us both great joy and sadness. That is the way we are hardwired and for good health, must honor our feelings.

One model suggests that all emotions arise from the 2 basic feelings of **love** and **fear**. According to Frank Sant'Agata all emotions can be traced back to these primary feelings.

"Love and fear are the only emotions we as human entities are able to express. All the others are just sub-categorical emotions. For example, on love's side there is joy, peacefulness, happiness, forgiveness, and a host of others. On the other hand, fear reflects hate, depression, guilt, inadequacy, discontentment, prejudice, anger, attack, and so on.

Love and fear cannot coexist. Where one is, the other can't be also. The one will leave immediately, should the other enter its presence. If you find yourself in a situation where you are experiencing great joy, and are suddenly overtaken by fear, the joy is gone! But it works the other way too: If you are terrorized, frightened, or otherwise threatened in any way, all you need to do is turn to the love within and the fears disappears."

Next time you are watching TV talk shows and the host is trying to convince you of something, evaluate their presentation using the following criteria: is this a manipulation of the fear and reward stick. Do as I say: good things will happen; if not, bad things will happen. *Most often, the media, politicians, some forms of religion and corporations continually use this manipulation.* Unless you see the manipulation...it is very difficult to understand and disarm, particularly, when you are up against a formidable societal power structure.

From a spiritual standpoint, we want to become masters of our emotions, so we can *temporarily* get beyond them. When we are emotionally charged, most often, the quiet, spiritual part of ourselves will not come forward. Generally it will not operate under these conditions.

Daily Practices to Counter Fear

OK, so now that you have me totally paranoid, and frightened about the end of the world, what am I supposed to do about all of this? Here are a few suggestions, from my personal toolbox on life, to help you conquer your fear reaction, and more easily access that quiet part of yourself which is more peaceful and serene.

- *Honor your Fear.* Express it in healthy ways — pray, kiss your children and be grateful for what you have. Ask the Universe/God to help you go beyond your fear and live a full life. *Offer up a prayer of gratitude/thankfulness* for what you do have and not what will be taken; turn to love and gratefulness. Ordinarily the mind is so constructed it can only keep one thought in it at a time.

- *Scenarios of the world ending are just that.* Scenarios or potentials. Unless we collectively change and live according to the Golden Rule this is one potential. Remember you can only control yourself and work to make your world/life better.

- *Lead a full Life.* Participate in the world; try to make it a better place. Travel to the different parts of yourself and follow one of the great spiritual paths to completion.

- *Live in the moment.* All you have is this moment; try to make it work and be joyous for you.

- *Happiness Calendar.* Every day do something small that makes you happy. Laugh, tell a joke; make a telephone call to your friends. Research tells us that happy people have many small things they look forward to each day.

- *NEWS Vacation.* Take a vacation from your computer, the television set and reportage of the bad things on the NEWS. Sit quietly or go for a walk; try to listen to that quiet part of yourself that knows where it is going.

- *Pray.* Make each moment a celebration to life and offer up a song of gratitude for the opportunity to be here.

- *Think Happy Thoughts.* And when you find yourself becoming sad, angry, confused, remember that from confusion comes order. One moment we are happy and the next sad. We have the capacity to create our own reality and a happy traveler thinks happy thoughts. Tell jokes, laugh, or watch a funny movie.

- *Avoid making comparisons* between yourself and others; particularly what they have and you do not have.

- *Monitor your expectations* about life and people. Often expectations are a trap that robs us of our happiness and peace of mind (i.e., I expected by this point in my life or if I followed this spiritual path, I would be free of pain).

- *Life can be glorious but remember it's a full-contact sport.* Chaos and order co-exist and are part of the Cosmic Plan.

- *Be with Positive People.* Be selective with the people you hang around and what they talk about. Positive and loving people are good medicine

- *Avoid Alcohol/Recreational Drugs.* Most are depressants and can affect your mood.

- *Balanced Living.* All things in moderation and strive to lead a complete, multi-level balanced life.

- *Replaying Old Tapes.* Avoid going over and over, troubling things that have happened. Some of this is necessary, but most often, we replay it too much.

Conclusions

The more we practice controlling our consciousness and awareness, and seeing the fear/reward manipulation about us, the easier it will become to think more tranquil thoughts. Then, one day we will experience what lies beyond emotions; and the higher consciousness will emerge.

Often for many events in life, we cannot control harmful outcomes; when something painful or chaotic occurs, we must feel and honor the pain. Yet experience teaches with a little hard work, we can limit fear and worry about potentials; all of us must learn to separate out what is a possibility, and learn to use the tools in our personal tool box to move past potentials and reach happier, more tranquil thoughts.

In 1969, it was during a BBC interview that Mrs. Beryl Worth, when questioned about her positive personal adjustment, to a recent potentially fatal diagnosis of cancer, answered in the following way.

"I think it was St. Ignatius who was sweeping the corridor and his novices came and said to him, 'If the world, if you knew the world were going to come to an end in 10 minutes, what would you do?' And he said, 'Go on sweeping the corridor.' And that is just what I'm going to do."

In every moment life is ending and beginning; life is joy and pain, chaos and peace. With every moment, after we have experienced what we need to experience; we must learn and remember to go on doing our work and 'continue sweeping the corridor.'

References

Idries Shah, *Knowing How to Know*, The Octagon Press, London, 1998, p. 152.

This quote appears online at Frank Sant'Agata, *On Love and Fear*, accessed 3/22/09: http://timelessmiracles.com/LightGuide/love.htm

Interview with Mrs. Beryl Worth shortly before her death. BBC transcript "I'll go on sweeping the corridor" June 1969. Appearing in and compiled by: Cecil, Rieu, and Wade, *The King's Son*, The Octagon Press: The Institute for Cultural Research, 1981, p. 162.

Other books by Stewart Bitkoff

- **Journey of Light: Trilogy**, Authorhouse, 2004.

- **A Commuter's Guide to Enlightenment**, Llewellyn, 2008.

- **Sufism for Western Seekers**, Abandoned Ladder, 2011.

- **The Ferryman's Dream**, Abandoned Ladder, 2012.

- **Beyond The River's Gate**, Abandoned Ladder, 2014.

- **The Appleseed Journal**, Abandoned Ladder, 2016.

- **Light On The Mountain**, Abandoned Ladder, 2016.

- **The World of Pond Stories**, Abandoned Ladder, 2018.

Books are available on Amazon.com in paperback and Kindle.

About the Author

Stewart Bitkoff grew up in New York City and spent most of his professional career living and working in the New York City area. An expert in therapeutic recreation and psychiatric rehabilitation and treatment, Dr. Bitkoff has been on the faculty or served as field instructor for multiple colleges and universities.

He has written work centering on the topic of the completed person and the original human development system. For years, Dr. Bitkoff studied in two modern mystical schools. Professionally he worked to help the mentally ill integrate their altered states of consciousness into the physical world; recently he worked with children and their families as a behavioral consultant.

Please visit his website at www.stewartbitkoff.com or visit on **Facebook**.

www.ingramcontent.com/pod-product-compliance
Lightning Source LLC
LaVergne TN
LVHW041541070426
835507LV00011B/853